Keyboard Capers

Rebecca Doyle Stout

07-1987

MUSIC THEORY FOR CHILDREN

ISBN # 0-89826-051-5

KEYBOARD CAPERS

Second Edition, May 1989

For further information write:

The Elijah Company
Rt. 2, Box 100-B
Crossville, TN 38555

Contents

Acknowledgements

Editor, Maxine McGill

Cover design, Guy Livingston

Drawings, Jenny Craven

Teaching Aids: The Music Train and Dynamic Ducks, Ellen Rash

Special appreciation to Pamela M. Reddoch for typing the manuscript.

Introduction

Keyboard Capers is written primarily to aid parents in teaching music theory to their children. The book contains over one hundred activities to help children master various aspects of music theory. It is not necessary for the home teacher to be familiar with music theory concepts in order to use this book successfully. In particular, home schooling parents will especially enjoy using Keyboard Capers as it allows them to assume responsibility for teaching rudimentary information to their child (children) in a manner that is designed to make learning music theory fun and easy.

The activities are basically designed for two participants although it is easy to make slight adjustments to accommodate one or two more players if necessary. In addition, many of the games may be used successfully in group theory classes of eight to ten students; often, simply supplying additional teaching aids (manipulatives) for each student is the only necessary change.

The book has a simple and straightforward format which makes it easy to use. Most activities require a minimum of preparation and many utilize the same teaching aids. A description of the teaching aids and directions for making them are found on pages 107 through 111. Also there are several "fun" pages which the student completes himself.

In order to use Keyboard Capers it is not necessary for the student to have begun lessons on a particular musical instrument; however, it is an especially ideal text to use with beginning piano students. A few activities require a piano to visually and aurally reinforce information but if a piano is not available an electric keyboard, xylophone, or other instrument can sometimes be substituted depending on the activity.

As the title suggests, Keyboard Capers is designed to make learning music theory a pleasant experience. Hopefully, it may spark an interest in music which will perhaps motivate the student to continue to broaden his appreciation for and knowledge of music.

Some Common Questions About Keyboard Capers

What is Keyboard Capers?

Keyboard Capers is not a book of musical compositions. It is not a book that teaches one to play a musical instrument. Keyboard Capers is a book about the components of music: notes, rhythm, musical words and signs, treble and bass clefs, chords, scales, key signatures, and basic ear training. In short, it is about music theory. It contains over 100 learning games and activities to teach and reinforce the musical concepts necessary to read and understand music.

Who can use Keyboard Capers?

Keyboard Capers can be used successfully by anyone who wants to teach rudimentary music theory to children ages 3 and up. The book was written primarily for parents, including those who have little or no knowledge of music theory, who want to introduce or reinforce musical concepts at home. It is ideal for parents who home school. The lesson plans provide instruction for 1 to 2 years of study and will give the student a broad, solid foundation in the basics of music theory. The child does not need to know how to play an instrument in order to master the concepts presented in Keyboard Capers.

Keyboard Capers is also ideal for parents whose child/children are beginning piano students, and is especially helpful to piano teachers, both traditional method and Suzuki* method. Since parental involvement is a cornerstone of the Suzuki method, the Suzuki piano instructor has the added advantage of making assignments to the parents for follow-up activities at home. In this way the instructor and parents may share the responsibility of teaching music theory.

Music teachers have had great success using Keyboard Capers with individual students or groups.

Must the student be able to play an instrument?

No. It is not necessary for the child to know how to play an instrument in order to master the concepts presented in Keyboard Capers.

Is a piano necessary?

There are approximately 25 activities which require some sort of keyboard. For families who do not own or have access to an acoustic (regular) piano, the popular

*"Suzuki" and "The Suzuki Method" are trademarks of Dr. Shinichi Suzuki and are exclusively licensed to the International Suzuki Association. Summy-Birchard is the sole authorized publisher for the world except Japan of the Suzuki Method materials.

portable keyboards will be sufficient. Only two activities, Two Frogs and Three Black Birds, require an 88 key piano, and these activities may be deleted if necessary.

If neither an acoustic nor a portable keyboard is available, excellent results can be achieved with a mallet instrument such as a xylophone. Even one as small as eight notes can be used for most of the ear training activities. Of all the activities that require an instrument, these are the most important. Developing the ear is an integral part of basic music theory, and these activities should not be neglected. Using a xylophone will necessitate omitting several of the remaining activities, but these activities primarily reinforce rather than introduce material.

How long is the course of instruction?

Depending on the age of the student and frequency of teaching, these lessons will provide approximately one to two years of instruction.

How often should Keyboard Capers be used?

It is possible to cover a minimum of one lesson per week; however, two or more are preferable. The teacher should allow thirty minutes for each lesson. Of course, the length will vary according to the age and attention span of the student.

What should be the age of the student?

Students may be as young as three years old and as old as ten or eleven. The only prerequisites to instruction with Keyboard Capers are: the student must be able to identify letters of the alphabet, and the student must recognize and be able to name the colors red, blue, purple, and pink. Keyboard Capers is of optimal use with the elementary grades, but may be used successfully with slightly older students if some of the activities are adapted to their ages and interests.

Can more than one student be taught at a time?

Keyboard Capers can be used one-on-one or with a class of students. When used with a music class, it is helpful to divide the students into groups with similar levels of musical training. There is a section immediately preceding the lesson plans which offers suggestions for group instruction using Keyboard Capers. Additional manipulatives may be necessary, such as extra game pieces and extra notes, depending on the size of the class.

Do I have to buy anything else to make Keyboard Capers complete?

The book contains patterns for all of the game pieces and manipulatives plus instructions for their assembly. However, for those who want to save preparation time, a manipulatives kit is available. This kit contains aids for all of the games and activities in Keyboard Capers. Each piece is professionally illustrated on heavy duty card stock and then laminated to withstand repeated use.

Suggestions For A Successful Learning Experience

To ensure meaningful and enjoyable learning experiences, be sure to preview each lesson before introducing it to the student. Although Keyboard Capers requires minimal preparation time before teaching, the teacher should be familiar with the concepts and have assembled any necessary teaching aids beforehand.

Present the material in an enthusiastic manner. Be prepared to respond with patience when the student's progress does not meet expectations. Be generous with praise when accomplishments, no matter how small, occur. Strive to end each lesson on a positive note before the student becomes tired, bored, or frustrated. This helps to ensure a positive attitude for both teacher and student.

Expect to repeat certain lessons as necessary and to switch activities to accommodate the student's needs and preferences. Each student will have his or her favorite games and may wish to review these more often than they are listed.

Remember that the purpose of Keyboard Capers is to make learning music theory fun and easy. Schedule and use the music lessons as a reprieve from or a reward for intensive efforts in other subjects, or use the music activities to "rejuvenate" a listless student.

Some students enjoy having a manuscript book in which they can compose their own music. As they progress through Keyboard Capers, even children who have never played a musical instrument are able to count out notes and rests for measures in all of the time signatures. They are then delighted to have their compositions played for them.

Finally, to build on this musical foundation, consider attending concerts with the student. Many concerts are designed specifically for the young listener and can often help to foster a lifelong appreciation of music.

Explanation of The Lesson Plans

The lesson plans for Keyboard Capers are divided into three sections: Section A, Section B, and Section C. Section A contains lessons from Chapter I of Keyboard Capers that acquaint the student with the musical alphabet and the sequence of the notes. All students must have mastered the skills in Chapter I before moving on in the book. Section B contains lessons that are specific to a piano or other keyboard. This section may be omitted if the student is not studying piano or does not have access to a piano or other keyboard. Section C contains lessons that continue instruction in music theory but do not necessarily require access to a piano or familiarity with a keyboard.

The lesson plans have been devised so that complimentary games, activities, or reviews are presented in the same lesson or same sequence of lessons.

Depending upon the student's familiarity with music, there are four ways in which the lesson plans can be used. These four ways are explained below:

Level 1: The student has had no previous musical training and is not taking piano lessons. He or she is unfamiliar with the alphabet skills found in Chapter I. The Level 1 student should first master Chapter I of Keyboard Capers according to the lesson plans in Section A. The Section B activities, which introduce the student to the piano keyboard, are optional. You may include these if a keyboard is available and the student is eager to learn some basic keyboard skills. (Most students enjoy the Two Frogs and Three Black Birds activities.) Otherwise, after Lesson 8 go directly to Lesson 24, the first lesson in Section C.

Level 2: The student has not had and is not taking music lessons, but has mastered the skills found in Chapter I. He or she will omit Section A. Section B, which is an orientation to the keyboard, is optional. Begin with these fun activities if a piano is available, otherwise begin with Section C.

Level 3: This is a beginning piano student who is in the process of mastering the skills in Chapter 1. This student should cover all three sections in order: Section A, then Sections B and C.

Level 4: This is a beginning piano student who has mastered the skills found in Chapter 1. This student should omit Section A. He or she should begin with Section B and continue through section C to the end of the book.

By following this sequence of instruction, the music theory in Keyboard Capers can be successfully taught in as few as 77 or as many as 100 lessons. Depending on the age of the student and frequency of sessions, the lesson plans will provide one to two years of instruction. Each lesson will take approximately thirty minutes.

Using Keyboard Capers With A Group of Students

Keyboard Capers produces excellent results when used with a group of students. It provides ample opportunity for student participation and "hands-on" classroom activity. It is helpful to divide the students in the class into two groups and follow the course of study suggested for each group.

Group 1: These students are unfamiliar with the skills found in Chapter 1. They will need to be taught the musical alphabet, beginning with Section A of the lesson plans. Section B, which is an orientation to the piano keyboard, is optional. Include these activities if a piano is available, otherwise omit Section B and go directly to Lesson 24, the first lesson in Section C. Continue with Section C to the end of the book.

Group 2: These students are familiar with the musical alphabet and the skills found in Chapter 1. They may omit Section A. Section B, which introduces the students to the piano keyboard, is optional, depending on the availability of a piano. If Section B is omitted, the students will begin their study in Keyboard Capers with Lesson 24, the first lesson in Section C.

The instructor can easily determine into which group each student belongs by playing some of the games in Chapter 1 such as "What's Missing?" or "Short Segments."

When teaching Keyboard Capers to a group, some of the teaching aids such as the definition and tempo cards may be enlarged so that they can be easily seen by all of the students. Teachers have also found it helpful to make the manipulatives out of very durable material and have them laminated. Extra game pieces, such as extra notes and rhythm cards, are also advisable.

Lesson Plans

SECTION A:

Lesson 1
Chapter I: Learning the Music Alphabet

Lesson 2
Chapter I: Learning the Music Alphabet - Review

Lesson 3
Chapter I: Learning the Music Alphabet - Review

Lesson 4
Chapter I: Learning the Music Alphabet - Review

Lesson 5
Chapter I: The Music Train

Lesson 6
Chapter I: The Music Train - Review

Lesson 7
Chapter I: The Music Train - Review

Lesson 8
Chapter I: Alphabet Hunt

Lesson 9
Chapter I: Alphabet Hunt - Review

Lesson 10
Chapter I: What's Missing?

Lesson 11
Chapter I: What's Missing? - Review

Lesson 12
Chapter I: Starting with Different Letters
Note: Remember that in the music alphabet A always follows G.

Lesson 13
Chapter I: Short Segments

Lesson 61
Chapter VI: Slap Down
Chapter VII: Tempo Markings

Lesson 62
Chapter VII: Dynamic Ducks - Review
Chapter VII: Stairsteps

Lesson 63
Chapter VII: Stairsteps - Review
Chapter VI: Note Spell
Note: Non-reading students may review Sad Cecil (Chapter VI).

Lesson 64
Chapter VI: Spell It
Note: Non-reading students may review Slap Down (Chapter VI).

Lesson 65
Chapter III: Ledger Lines
Chapter VII: Fling'em

Lesson 66
Chapter VI: Naming Ledger Lines I

Lesson 67
Chapter VI: Name This Note I
Chapter VII: Oops!

Lesson 68
Chapter VII: Oops! - Review
Chapter VI: Fun Page - Treble Clef Notes

Lesson 69
Chapter III: The Bass Clef and Staff
Chapter VII: Hocus Focus

Lesson 70
Chapter VI: Just Lines
Note: Use the bass clef staff to introduce the bass clef line notes.
Also, use the bass clef staff in Lessons 71 through 74.

Lesson 71
Chapter VII: Hocus Focus - Review
Chapter VI: Just Spaces

Lesson 72
Chapter VI: Sad Cecil

Lesson 73
Chapter VI: Lines and Spaces Together

Lesson 74
Chapter VI: Connecting the Staff to the Keyboard
Chapter VI: Reviewing the Lines and Spaces

Lesson 75
Chapter V: Half Steps - Brief review
Chapter V: Whole Steps - Brief review
Chapter IX: Pentachords

Lesson 76
Chapter IX: Pentachords - Review
Note: Introduce the pentachords starting on D, E, F, A, and B.
Chapter VI: Fun Page - Bass Clef Trucks

Lesson 77
Chapter IX: Pentachords - Review
Note: Introduce the pentachords starting Db, Eb, Gb, Ab, and Bb.
Chapter VI: Matches
Note: Use bass clef staff cards.

Lesson 78
Chapter VI: Slap Down
Note: Use bass clef staff cards.

Lesson 79
Chapter IX: Major Scales

Lesson 80
Chapter IX: Major Scales - Review
Note: Build scales beginning on D, A, and E.
Chapter VI: Naming Ledger Line Notes II

Lesson 81
Chapter IX: Major Scales - Review
Note: Build scales beginning on B, F#, and C#.

Lesson 82
Chapter VI: Fun Page - Bass Clef Notes
Chapter IX: Focus on Key Signatures

Lesson 83
Chapter IX: Roll and Name Key Signatures
Note: Review scales beginning on G, D, A, E, B, F#, and C#.

Lesson 84
Chapter IX: Key Signature Slap Down
Note: Review the scales having sharps in the key signature.

Lesson 85
Chapter VIII: Introducing the Intervals of a Major Scale
Chapter IX: Fun Page - Sharps on the Staff

Lesson 86
Chapter VIII: Major Seconds and Major Thirds
Chapter IX: Fun Page - Major Scales I

Lesson 87
Chapter VIII: Major Seconds, Major Thirds, Perfect Fourths and Perfect Fifths
Chapter IX: Fun Page - Key Signatures I

Lesson 88
Chapter VIII: Major Sixths, Major Sevenths, and Perfect Octaves

Lesson 89
Chapter VIII: Interval Scramble

Lesson 90
Chapter IX: Scales with Flats in the Key Signature

Lesson 91
Chapter IX: Roll and Name Key Signatures
Note: Review scales beginning on F, Bb, Eb, Ab, Db, Gb, and Cb.

Lesson 92
Chapter IX: Roll and Name Key Signatures - Review
Chapter VIII: Interval Scramble - Review

Lesson 93
Chapter VIII: Interval Scramble - Review
Chapter IX: Fun Page - Flats on the Staff

Lesson 94
Chapter IX: Key Signature Slap Down
Note: Review scales containing flats.

Chapter I: THE MUSIC ALPHABET

The very young student is often in the process of learning the alphabet when he begins music lessons. The teacher must determine if the student can identify the letters of the music alphabet (A, B, C, D, E, F, and G), say them in order, and identify missing letters. Also, the student should be able to identify short segments, say the letters in order starting with letters other than A, and say the alphabet backward.

The activities in this Chapter are designed to make mastering these skills fun and easy. Many times a student will ask to play his favorite games again and again.

Remember to introduce new activities at a pace which is comfortable for the student to help him establish a positive attitude toward learning.

Learning the Music Alphabet

PURPOSE: To practice recognizing the letters of the music alphabet.

TEACHING AIDS: Several alphabet cards - A's, B's, and C's (later, add remaining letters)

DIRECTIONS: Sit on the floor facing one another. Keep one A, B, and C for yourself. Scatter the remaining cards face up on the floor in front of the student.

Hold up the A as you say "A" several times. Place the card on the floor facing the student.

"Do you see an A among your cards?"

As the student finds the matching cards, encourage him to say "A" as he places each card on top of your A.

Hold up the B. "Can you say 'B' with me? That's good!"

Place the B to the right (from the student's perspective) of the stack of A's.

Encourage the student to find all of his matching letters and place them in a stack on top of your B.

Continue in the same manner with C.

In the first session you may want to introduce only three letters. Add the remaining letters, one or two at a time in later sessions, until the student recognizes all seven.

The Music Train

PURPOSE: To have fun identifying the letters of the music alphabet and placing them in order.

TEACHING AID: The music train

DIRECTIONS: Scatter the train cars on the floor. Place the engine in front of and to the left of the seated student.

Help the student to locate the car with an A showing on its side. Place it to the right of the engine. "What letter comes after A? Yes, B." "Hook" that car to the first one.

Continue in this manner until the train is completed.

Point to each car as, together, you and the student say the letters in order.

NOTE: "The Music Train" is one of three teaching aids in this book which requires a significant amount of preparation; however, once finished, the train may be substituted as the teaching aid for other activities such as "ALPHABET HUNT" and "NAMING THE ALPHABET BACKWARD."

Children delight in playing with the brightly colored music train. The investment of time in making this teaching aid, while optional, may help to make learning the music alphabet even more fun.

Alphabet Hunt

PURPOSE: To have fun identifying the letters of the music alphabet and saying them in order.

TEACHING AIDS: One set of alphabet cards and an Easter basket (or suitable container)

NOTE: The music train may be substituted as the teaching aid in this activity.

DIRECTIONS: Have the student wait in another room as you hide the alphabet cards much like you would hide eggs for an indoor Easter egg hunt. When the cards are hidden, call the student into the room.

"I'll bet you have never been on an alphabet hunt. I have hidden seven alphabet cards around the room. Here is your basket for collecting the cards. Now let's see how many cards you can find!"

When all the cards are located, sit on the floor with the student. Take the A from his basket and place it on the floor in front of him. Say the name of the letter together.

"Can you find the letter B in your basket?" Gently guide the student to the correct card, if necessary. Place the B to the right of A. Encourage the student to say the letters in order with you.

Follow the same procedure with the remaining letters until all the cards are in order. Starting with A, point to each card as, together, you and the student name them aloud several times.

What's Missing?

PURPOSE: To reinforce the identification and order of the music alphabet.

TEACHING AID: One set of alphabet cards

DIRECTIONS: Tell the student that you are going to hand him the set of alphabet cards but it is possible that one or more cards might be missing.

Encourage him to lay the cards in order as quickly as possible but to be sure to let you know as soon as he realizes a letter is missing and which one it is.

Once the student has identified the missing letter(s), gather the cards and have him close his eyes as you again remove one or two cards. Sometimes do not remove any cards.

Ask him to open his eyes as you hand him the cards so that he may play the game again.

Starting With Different Letters

PURPOSE: To practice naming the music alphabet beginning with different letters.

TEACHING AID: One set of alphabet cards

DIRECTIONS: Sit on the floor with the student. Hold the alphabet cards as you would a hand of playing cards. Have the student select one card and place it on the floor in front of him. This card determines the order.

Next, place the remaining cards around him face up on the floor. See how quickly he can locate and place in order the remaining cards.

When the cards are in order say them aloud together from the beginning.

As soon as one round is completed, gather the cards and begin again.

Short Segments

PURPOSE: To practice naming short segments of the alphabet.

TEACHING AIDS: Three sets of alphabet cards

DIRECTIONS: Divide the cards into seven groups of three cards each. The examples will be A B C, D E F, G A B, C D E, F G A, B C D, and E F G.

Place these groups on the floor leaving the second or third (or both) cards face down as shown below:

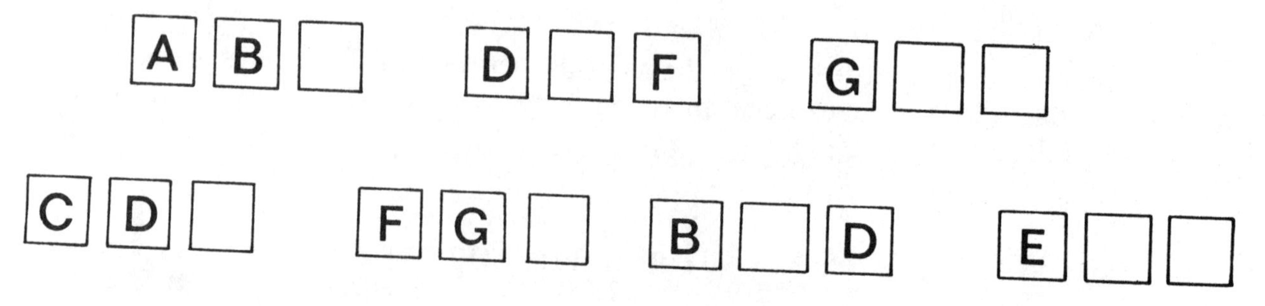

Point to the face-up cards in the first group as you and the student say them aloud. Have the student name the face-down card before turning it over to confirm his answer.

Continue in this manner with the remaining groups.

To make the activity more challenging, change the order of the seven groups each time you play.

Naming The Alphabet Backward

PURPOSE: To practice thinking and saying the alphabet backward.

TEACHING AID: One set of alphabet cards (or use the music train as a substitute)

DIRECTIONS: Sit on the floor with the student. Place a G in front of and to the right of him and scatter the remaining cards on the floor.

"What letter comes just before G? That's right, F. Let's find F and place it to the left of G. Now, what letter comes before F? Right again, E!"

Continue in the same manner until all cards are in order.

Practice naming them aloud together beginning with G. (You will be reading the cards from right to left in the same order as the keys are found on the piano.)

For more practice gather the cards and hold them as you would a hand of playing cards.

Have the student select one card, identify the letter, and place it to his right.

Scatter the remaining cards around the student and ask him to line them up backward, starting with the card he selected and working to the left, card by card.

Say the letters aloud together starting on the right and reading to the left.

Repeat the entire activity several times.

Win A Letter

PURPOSE: To practice naming the letters before and after a particular letter with visual help and then by memory.

TEACHING AIDS: Two sets of alphabet cards

DIRECTIONS: Hold one set of alphabet cards as you would a hand of playing cards. Have the student place the other set in front of him in order from A to G.

Ask the student to select one card from your hand, identify it, and place it just above his cards.

Encourage him to scan his cards and find the letter which precedes the letter he selected. Have him place that card to the left of the selected card. Have him find the letter which follows the selected card and place it to the right.

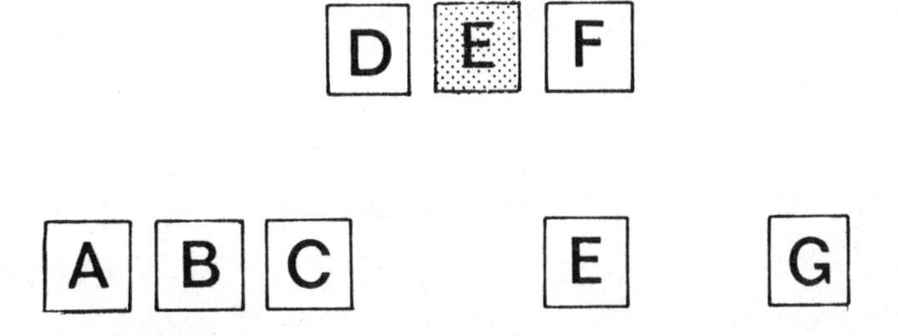

Each time the student correctly identifies both letters he wins and keeps the card which he selected from your hand and returns his cards to their original position. In the case of an incorrect identification, return the selected card to your hand and tell him he will have another opportunity to win that card.

To make the game more challenging, simply hold a set of alphabet cards as you would a hand of cards. Have the student choose and identify one card, then name orally the preceding and following letters.

As before, the game continues until the student wins all of your cards.

The Alphabet Race

PURPOSE: To have fun reinforcing all of the skills introduced in this Chapter.

TEACHING AIDS: Two sets of alphabet cards plus an extra C and two extra A's and B's, two spools of thread (or other objects to represent each player), a die (purchase this where games are sold), and several pennies

NOTE: Two or more players may participate. Also, you may lengthen the game by using more alphabet cards as you wish.

DIRECTIONS: Line up the cards as shown in the diagram, leaving some cards face down as you choose. The order of the cards on the top row should read from A through G plus A, B, and C. The cards on the bottom row should read from A through G plus an A and B (reading from left to right).

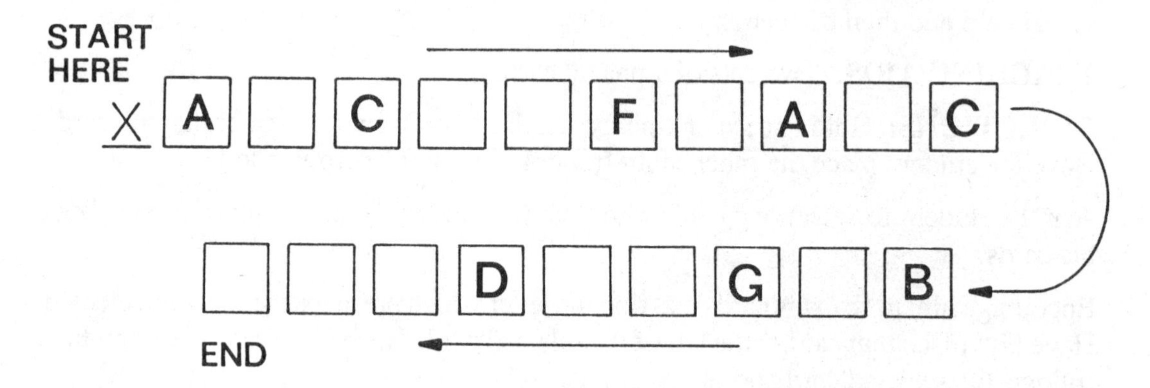

Both players place their spools at the starting point.

Each player rolls the die. The player rolling the highest number takes the first turn. If a tie occurs, roll again.

The player who goes first rolls the die again and moves his spool the indicated number of cards.

If the player's spool lands on an alphabet card which is face up, he simply needs to correctly identify that letter to earn a penny. If the player's spool lands on a face-down card, he must correctly identify that letter before turning it over. A correct identification of a face-down card earns the player three pennies. If the answer is correct, the card remains face up; however, if the letter is incorrectly identified, the card is returned face down.

There are no extra rolls earned as a result of a correct answer, rather, the turn simply rotates to the other player(s).

The first player to land on the last alphabet card in an exact roll of the die is the winner. Each player counts his pennies and the one having the most goes first the next time the game is played. In case of a tie, use the die to determine the order of turns as you did originally.

Chapter II: ORIENTATION

Even before formal lessons have begun, most beginning piano students have explored the keyboard, delighting in the many combinations of pitches which produce often unexpected sounds and occasionally, a recognizable melody.

Identifying patterns, differentiating between high and low registers, and naming, at random, any white key are skills the beginning pianist will enjoy learning.

Finger Number Names

PURPOSE: To introduce the finger number names.

TEACHING AIDS: None

DIRECTIONS: Sit beside the student and hold your hands out in front of you. Instruct the student to do the same.

"To play the piano we need to learn our finger number names. Our thumbs are number one. Can you wiggle fingers number one with me? Great! The pointer fingers are number two. Next come fingers number three. We sometimes call that finger 'long man' don't we? Our ring fingers are number four and the 'pinkies' are number five."

"Now, let's play a silly game. I will instruct you to place certain fingers on different parts of your body and I will play along with you. We will see how well we know our finger number names. Place fingers number two on your nose. Good! Remove them and place fingers number one on top of your head. Right! Don't we look silly like this? Okay, place fingers number five on your knees."

Continue in this manner to review each finger number name. Encourage the student to give some of the instructions himself.

Fun Page - Finger Number Names

PURPOSE: To have fun reviewing the finger number names.

TEACHING AIDS: Crayons

DIRECTIONS: Color each finger as directed below:

Fingers #1 - red

Fingers #2 - yellow

Fingers #3 - blue

Fingers #4 - green

Fingers #5 - orange

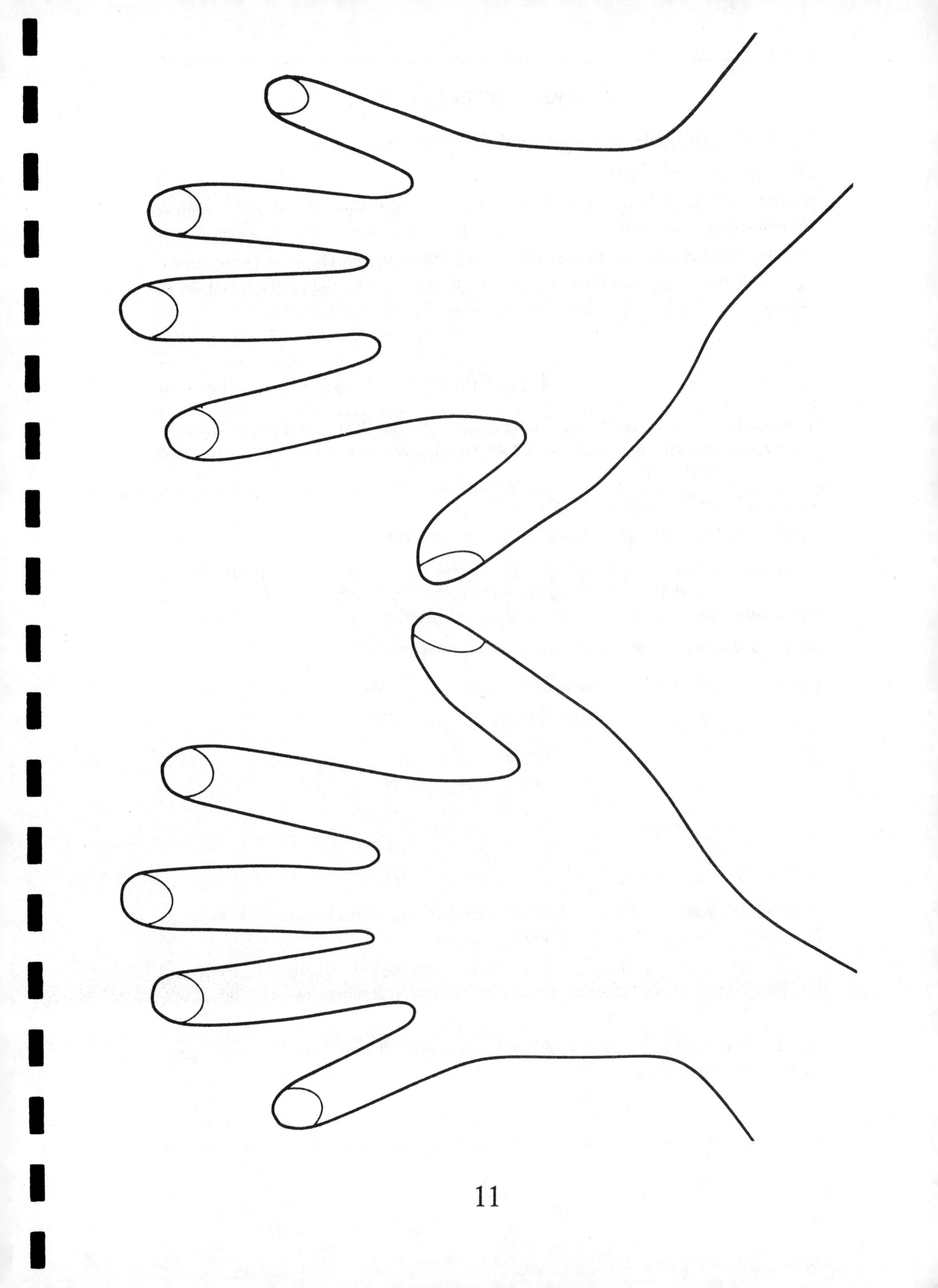

New Friends

PURPOSE: To practice naming the white keys in order.

TEACHING AID: A piano

DIRECTIONS: Starting with A, the lowest key on the piano, play and say the names of all the white keys in order. Encourage the student to say the names with you. Emphasize that A follows each G on the keyboard as one ascends.

Ask the student to play and say the names of the white keys before each home practice session for one week. Suggest that he use finger number 2 of the right hand.

Two Frogs

PURPOSE: To have fun finding all the groups of two black keys and to introduce the concept that to move to the right on the keyboard is to move upward and to move to the left is to move downward.

TEACHING AID: A piano

DIRECTIONS: Stand at the keyboard with the student.

Locate the lowest group of two black keys and play each note singly (from left to right) using fingers 2 and 3 of the right hand. Jump to the next group of two black keys and play them in the same manner. Continue to the highest group.

Say the following rhyme as you ascend - one word per note.

Two	frogs
climb	up
black	keys
with	ease
to	the
top	they
go	Oh!

Keep the note you play as you say "Oh" down as you ask, "What do you think the frogs do when they get to the top? They hop back down."

Starting with the highest group of two black keys, play the keys simultaneously as you say "hop." Play the remaining six groups in the same manner as you say "hop, hop, hop, hop, back down." (One word per group.)

Encourage the student to play "Two Frogs" as you say the rhyme. Have him use fingers 2 and 3 of the right hand.

Three Black Birds

PURPOSE: To familiarize the student with the pattern of three black keys and to reinforce the concept of low and high registers.

TEACHING AID: A piano

DIRECTIONS: Stand with the student at the keyboard.

Starting with the lowest group of three black keys, play each note singly from left to right, using fingers 2, 3, and 4 of the right hand. Jump to the next group of three black keys playing them in the same manner and continue to the highest group. To descend, repeat the highest group, reversing the order (from right to left), and continue until you return to and once again play the lowest group.

Following, is a rhyme to say as you play "Three Black Birds" (one word per note).

Ascending:

Three	black	birds
on	the	ground
flap	their	wings
up	ward	bound
chirp	chirp	chirp
fly	fly	fly
up	so	high

Descending:

Three	black	birds
up	so	high
flap	their	wings
down	they	fly
chirp	chirp	chirp
go	go	go
down	so	low

Encourage the student to say the rhyme with you as you play.

Next, let the student play as you say the rhyme. Suggest that he use fingers 2, 3, and 4 of the right hand. Do not necessarily attempt to correct what, at first, might be erratic fingering; the priorities are for the student to locate the groups of black keys and to have fun learning the rhyme.

Earn A Penny

PURPOSE: To practice identifying keys at the piano.

TEACHING AIDS: A piano and several pennies

DIRECTIONS: Place a penny on each C. (Remeber that the highest key on the piano is a C also.) Help the student to identify the lowest C in relation to the neighboring group of two black keys. Continue to emphasize this pattern with the remaining C's until the student can easily identify each C on his own.

Remove the pennies and practice locating other keys in relation to the groups of black keys. For instance, locate and name all of the F's, all of the E's, etc. Finally, for review, select several keys you wish the student to name and place one penny on each key. Explain to him that he may earn the pennies by correctly identifying the keys.

Keyboard Capers

PURPOSE: To have fun locating keys on the piano.

TEACHING AIDS: One set of alphabet cards and a piano

DIRECTIONS: Stand at the keyboard with the student.

Explain that you will place one alphabet card at a time on the music rack. You may, for example, ask him to locate three C's, or a low A and a high A, or all of the G's as you place the corresponding alphabet card in front of him.

Encourage the student to locate the keys as quickly as possible. Keep the game moving at a brisk pace and vary your instructions with each letter.

Chapter III: THE STAFF AND OTHER SIMPLE NOTATION

The activities in this Chapter are designed to introduce the student to simple notation. He will also add several new terms to his music vocabulary and learn to differentiate between line and space notes.

The Staff And Treble Clef

PURPOSE: To introduce the student to the staff and treble clef.

TEACHING AIDS: None

DIRECTIONS: Study together the illustration shown below. Point to each item as you explain it.

"How many lines do you see? That's right, five. How many spaces are between the lines? Yes, four. The five lines and four spaces are called the staff. Later we will find notes written on the staff."

"The treble clef tells us to play with the right hand." (You will have an opportunity to explain further the function of the treble clef in a later activity.)

Have the student pretend he is the teacher and describe the staff and explain the function of the treble clef to you.

Fun Page - The Treble Clef

PURPOSE: To practice drawing the treble clef.

TEACHING AID: A pencil

DIRECTIONS: Using the illustration on the next page, have the student trace the dotted lines and then draw several treble clefs on the lower staff.

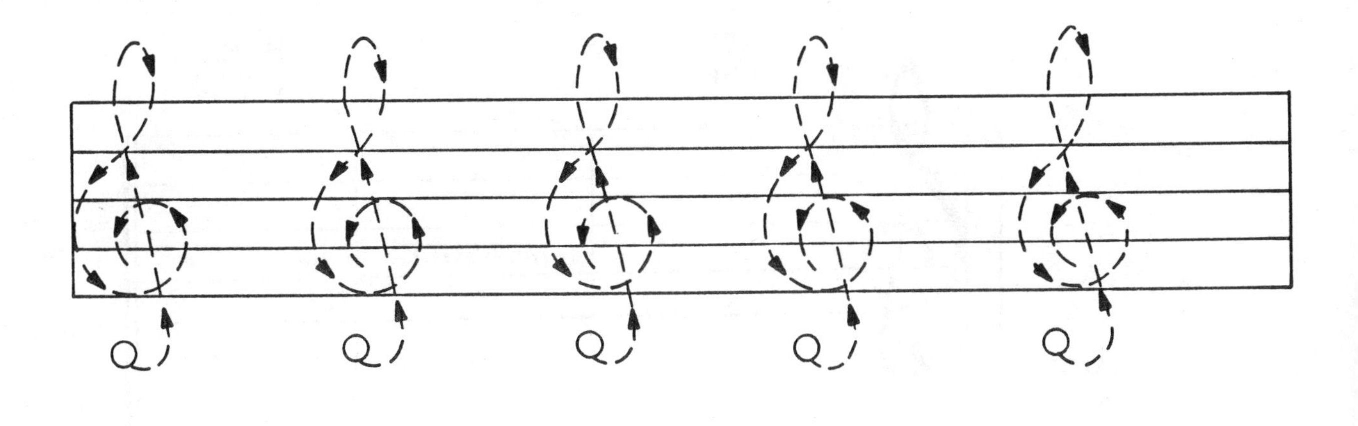

Review And New

PURPOSE: To review the staff and treble clef and to introduce the grand staff, brace, bass clef, measures, bar lines, and the double bar line.

TEACHING AID: One of the student's piano books

DIRECTIONS: Study together the illustration shown on the next page. Point to each item as you explain it.

"We have talked about the staff and the treble clef. Today I would like to introduce you to the bass clef. The bass clef tells us to play with the left hand. The combination of the treble and bass staffs (or staves) is called the grand staff, which is indicated by the brace. The bar lines divide the staff into measures. The double bar line is found only at the end of a piece of music."

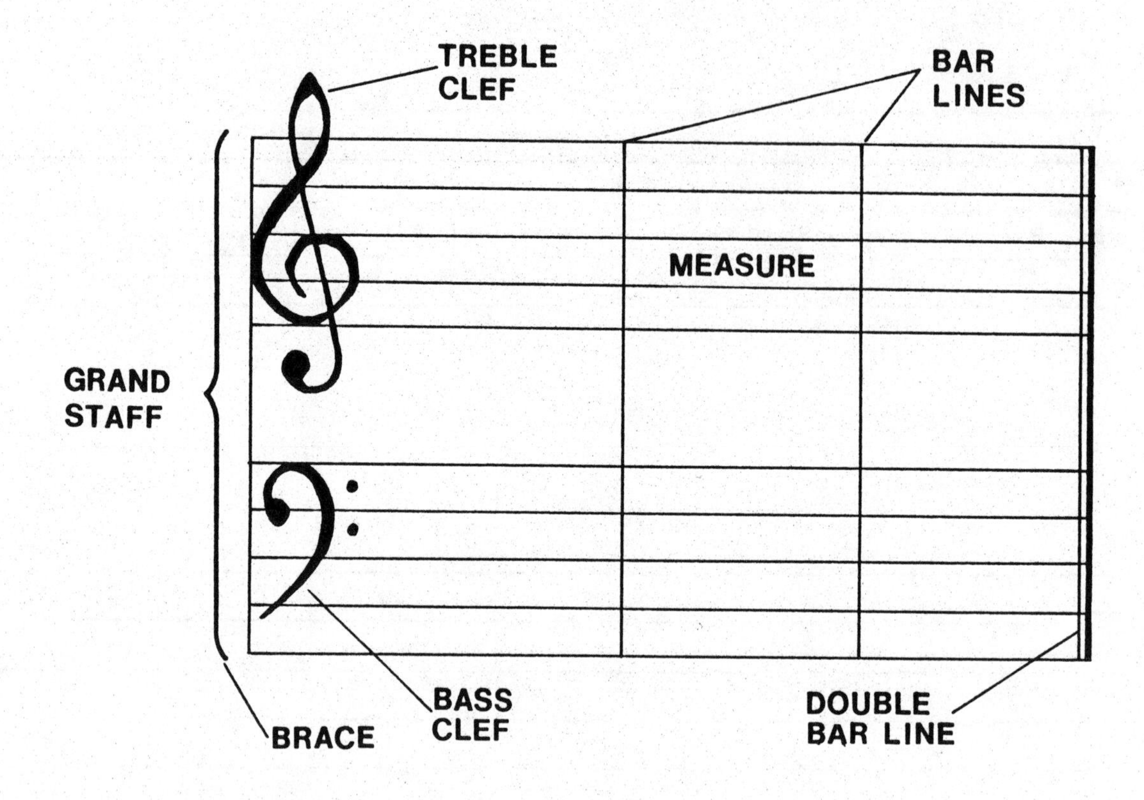

To reinforce these new terms and notations, scan together the pages of the music book. Have the student point to and identify these items as he recognizes them in the compositions.

Fun Page - The Bass Clef

PURPOSE: To practice drawing the bass clef.

TEACHING AID: A pencil

DIRECTIONS: Using the illustration on the next page, the student should trace the dotted lines, fill in the circles and then draw several bass clefs on the lower staff.

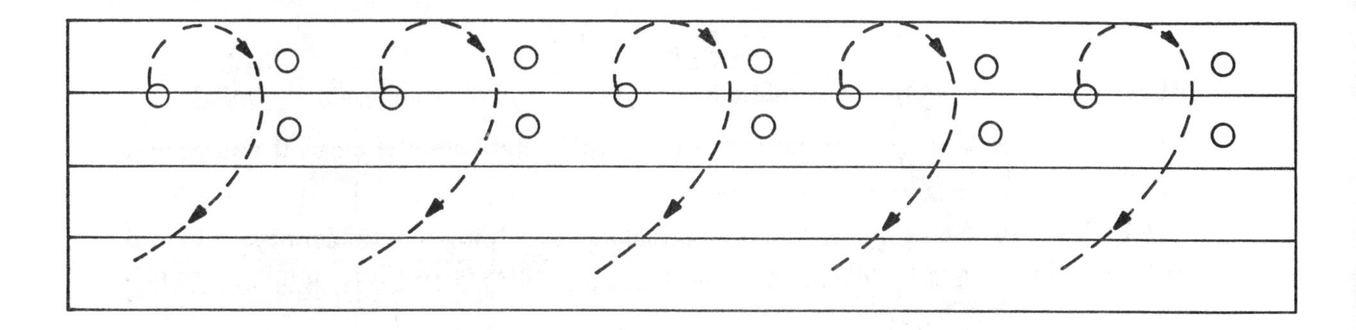

Line And Space Notes

PURPOSE: To help the student differentiate between line and space notes.

TEACHING AIDS: A one-staff board and plain notes

DIRECTIONS: Place a note on the lowest line as you say "line." Push it to the remaining four lines, stopping on each one to reinforce the word line.

"Do you notice that when I place the note on a line, the line seems to go exactly through the center of the note? Notes that have a line running through their center are called line notes."

Let the student practice placing the note on different lines. Praise him each time he positions the note correctly.

Next, take the note and place it on the lowest space as you say "space." Move the note to the remaining three spaces as you and the student say "space" together. Let the student practice moving the note to the different spaces.

Lastly, place several notes on the staff. Point to each one and have the student identify it as a line or a space note.

Repeat this last step several times.

Win A Card

PURPOSE: To have fun distinguishing between line and space notes.

TEACHING AIDS: Fifteen staff cards (Use treble and bass clef cards if you wish--avoid ledger line notes.)

DIRECTIONS: Show the student one card at a time helping him to identify each note as either a line or space note. Remind him that line notes have a line running through the center of the note.

Next, shuffle the staff cards. Decide between the two of you who will be the "space" person and who will be the "line" person.

Place three cards side by side face up on the floor. Have the student identify each note as either a line note or space note. If there are more line notes, the "line" person wins and collects all three cards and vice versa.

Play four more rounds with the remaining twelve cards.

Fun Page - Line Notes

PURPOSE: To practice identifying line notes.

TEACHING AIDS: Crayons

DIRECTIONS: The student is to color only the line notes.

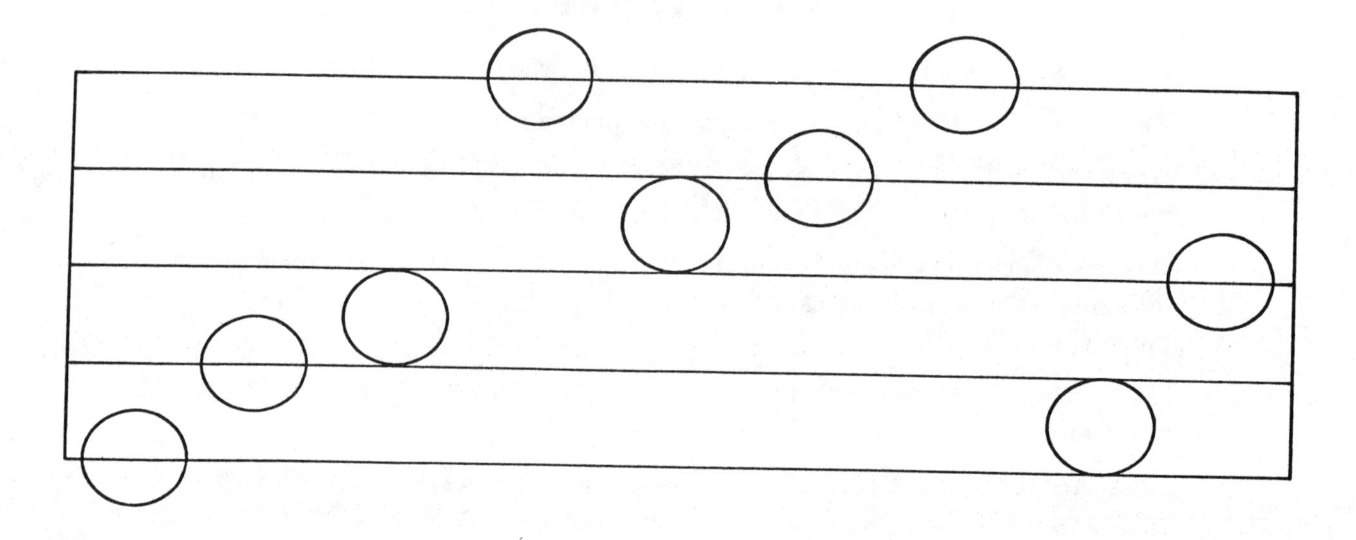

Fun Page - Space Notes

PURPOSE: To practice identifying space notes.

TEACHING AIDS: Crayons

DIRECTIONS: The student is to color only the space notes.

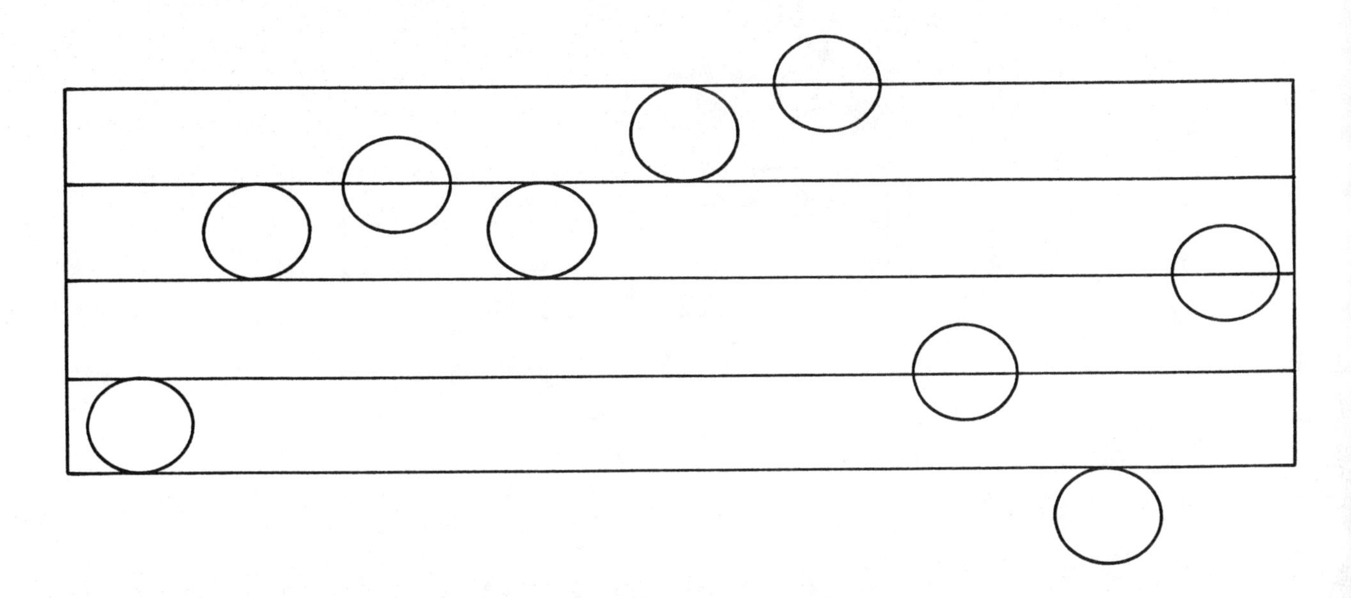

Ledger Lines

PURPOSE: To introduce the student to ledger line notes.

TEACHING AIDS: A two-staff board, five popsicle sticks (or similar objects) and a music book

DIRECTIONS: Place the popsicle sticks on the staff as shown on the next page:

"These short lines, represented by popsicle sticks, are called ledger lines. These lines help to expand the staff. Notes found on these extra lines are either higher (point to high ledger lines) or lower (point to low ledger lines) than the regular staff with the exception of one line. There is one ledger line which the staves share, which is middle C." (If a piano is close by, take the student to the piano and locate middle C together.)

"Now, let's look at the music book." Scan the pages together seeing who can find the most ledger line notes on any given page.

Chapter IV: RHYTHM

Students especially enjoy rhythmic activities. They respond enthusiastically to the colorful notes introduced in this Chapter and enjoy clapping and saying the rhythmic patterns with the teacher. Taking rhythmic dictation, learning about time signatures, and fitting rhythms into measures are other activities found in the Chapter as well.

Students master the information and skills regarding rhythm with great ease, creating a positive attitude toward learning to count and a greater appreciation for the importance of rhythmic accuracy.

Pinks And Purples

PURPOSE: To introduce the student to simple rhythmic patterns.

TEACHING AIDS: Pink and purple rhythm cards

DIRECTIONS: Place four pink notes on the floor side by side.

"What color are these notes? Yes, pink."

Point to each card from left to right as you say, "pink...pink...pink...pink."
Encourage the student to repeat this with you.

Exchange the second and fourth cards for two purple - note cards.

"Now, I have pink and purple notes. Let's say the rhythm together as I point to it -- 'pink ...purple... pink...purple'." Keep a steady pulse as you say it together.

"Let's add three more pink notes. Now we have pink...purple...pink...purple...pink...pink...pink."

Gather the cards and hand them to the student. "I'll bet you could make up your own rhythm!"

Let the student practice "writing" different patterns. Always point to the cards as, together, you and the student say the rhythms.

When the student is comfortable saying the words, suggest that both of you clap the rhythms as you say them together. Clap once to indicate a pink note and twice for a purple note--one clap per syllable.

NOTE: Rhythm cards, arranged in random order, will not necessarily create metric consistency.

Blue-oos Too

PURPOSE: To introduce the half note.

TEACHING AIDS: Pink, purple, and blue (only half notes, not dotted-half notes) rhythm cards

NOTE: "OO" rhymes with blue.

DIRECTIONS: Place a blue-note card in front of the student.

"What color is our newest note? Right, blue." Explain that this note will be called a "blue-oo." "When we see this note we will clap our hands as we say 'blue' and, leaving them clasped, simply bounce them once as we say 'oo'."

Shown on the next page are several sample rhythmic patterns.

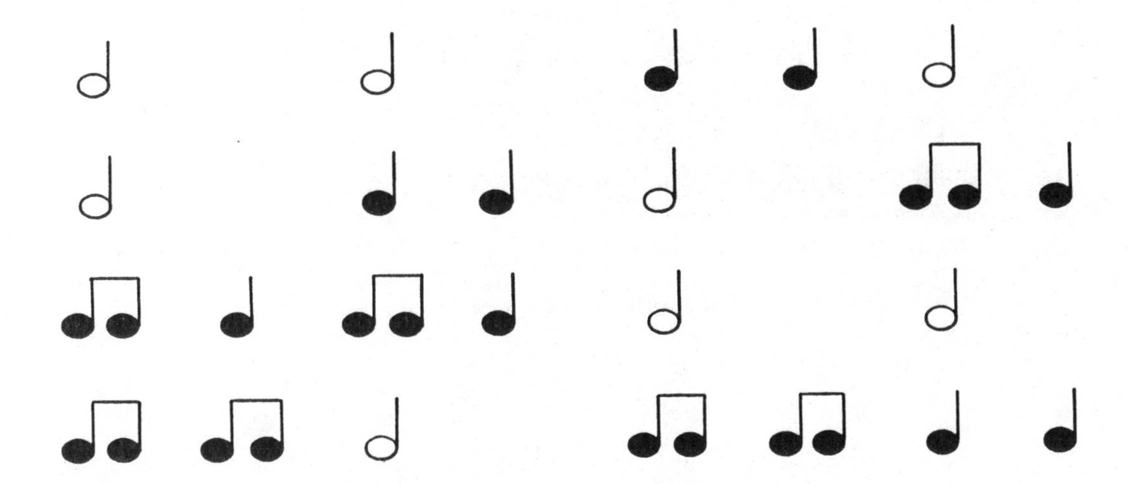

Clap and say the patterns together and create more of your own.

Soon, even the youngest students will be clapping and saying the rhythms with ease.

NOTE: It is not necessary to refer to the notes as quarter, eighth, or half notes yet; the true names will be introduced later.

Rhythmic Dictation

PURPOSE: To provide the student with an opportunity to write rhythmic patterns which he hears.

TEACHING AIDS: Pink, purple, and blue (only half notes) rhythm cards

DIRECTIONS: Sit with the student on the floor. Explain that you will clap in a manner that is indicative of a pink, purple, or blue-oo note. The student is to identify the type of note by your clap.

When the student has identified the three different notes by your clapping, ask him to listen and to watch you very carefully. Clap a short pattern such as pink...pink...purple...pink. Instruct the student to clap that same pattern back to you. If the pattern is incorrect, ask him to listen again. When he accurately repeats the rhythm ask him to "write" it using the rhythm cards. Gently guide him to the correct response, if necessary.

Finally, clap and say the rhythm together.

Repeat this activity over a period of time. Gradually, and as the student is ready, make the patterns slightly longer and incorporate all three note values.

Some sample patterns are shown on the next page:

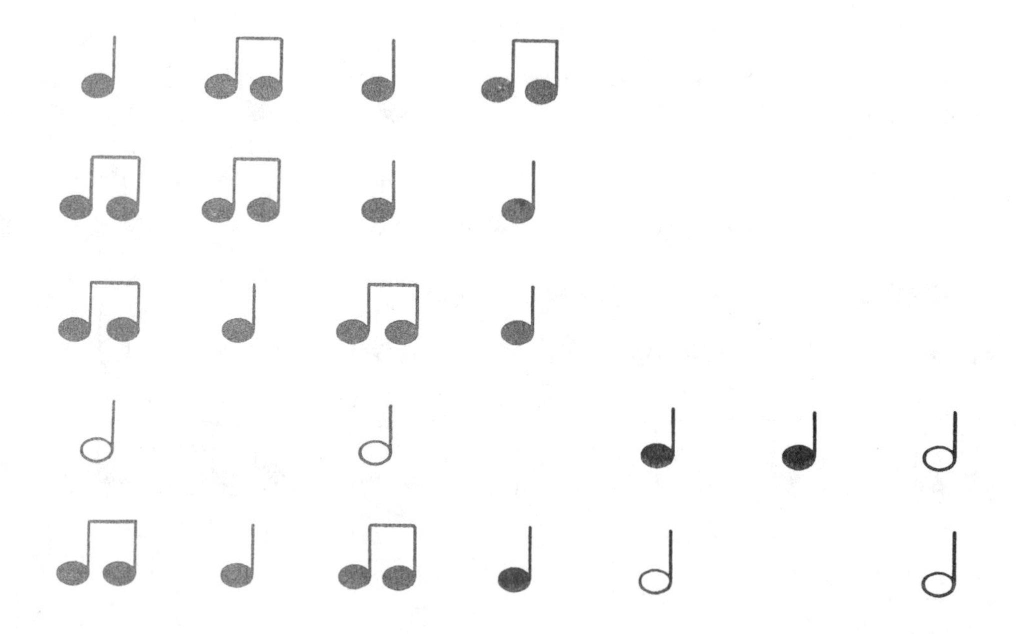

Look And Listen

PURPOSE: To practice identifying a rhythmic pattern visually.

TEACHING AIDS: Pink, purple, and blue (only half notes) rhythm cards

DIRECTIONS: Using only pink- and purple-note cards, lay two patterns on the floor, one above the other.

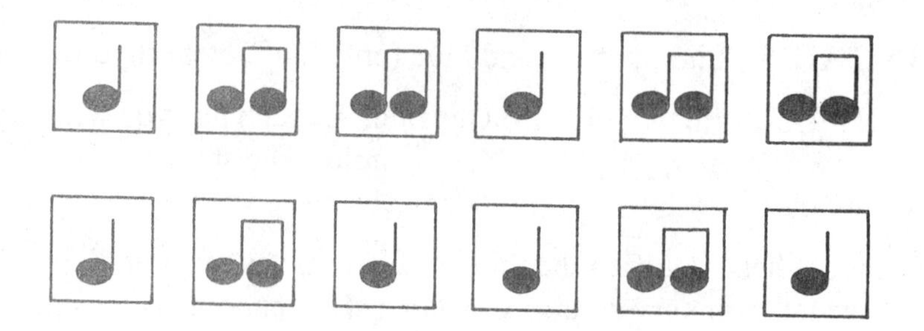

Clap one of the patterns two times. The first time, the student will listen and follow visually the upper example; the second time, he will look at the lower pattern and then identify which pattern he heard.

Repeat this activity several times using only pink- and purple-note cards, but soon, begin to include the blue-note cards as well.

Limit the patterns to five or six notes making the differences between them more and more subtle according to the student's readiness.

For fun, let the student write two patterns and clap one of them as you "contemplate" which pattern you heard!

Blue-oo Dots

PURPOSE: To introduce the dotted-half note.

TEACHING AIDS: Pink, purple, blue-oo, and blue-oo-dot rhythm cards

DIRECTIONS: Hold up a blue-oo and a blue-oo-dot card.

"How are these notes alike? That's right. Both have stems and the notes are not filled in. Now, what is the difference? Yes, that's easy. One has a dot. We will call that note a blue-oo dot." "To indicate that note we will clap as we say 'blue' and, leaving our hands clasped, we will bounce them as we say 'oo' and again as we say 'dot'."

To practice clapping you might write this pattern:

Take turns writing different patterns and, as always, clap and say them together.

Red-ed-ed-ed

PURPOSE: To introduce the whole note.

TEACHING AIDS: Rhythm cards (excluding the quarter rest)--all colors

DIRECTIONS: Hold up a red-note card and say to the student, "I would like to introduce you to my friend Ed. Tell me what color Ed is. Right, red. For fun, we will call him 'red-ed-ed-ed'!"

Demonstrate for the student how to indicate a red note. Clap as you say "red" and bounce your clasped hands on each "ed."

Practice a few simple patterns using whole notes and one or two other types of notes.

Gradually make the patterns more challenging by lengthening them and incorporating all types of notes.

Encourage the student to write his own patterns as you clap and say them together.

A Rest

PURPOSE: To introduce the quarter rest.

TEACHING AIDS: Pink and purple rhythm cards and quarter-rest cards

DIRECTIONS: Explain that a rest tells us to do exactly that--rest! A rest is a signal of silence.

Write the pattern shown below:

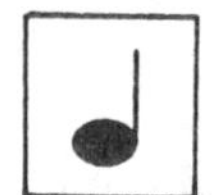  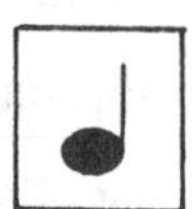   

Explain that since a rest is a symbol of silence, rather than clap, you will make a fist with each hand and say "rest" to indicate that sign. (I find that when children try to whisper the word rest, they sometimes take too much time, which interrupts the rhythmic stability of the pulse.)

Clap and say the rhythm shown above and then encourage the student to clap and say it with you.

Take turns creating different patterns using quarter rests. Always clap and say the rhythms together.

Gradually begin to include the other notes (half, dotted-half and whole) in the patterns as well.

Rainbows

PURPOSE: To have fun reviewing the various types of notes and the quarter rest.

TEACHING AIDS: Rhythm cards (including quarter rests) - all colors

DIRECTIONS: Scatter the cards on the floor.

"Let's build a rainbow with our colorful notes."

Begin choosing cards and laying them in an arc. The student will be quick to help you.

A sample "rainbow" is shown on the next page.

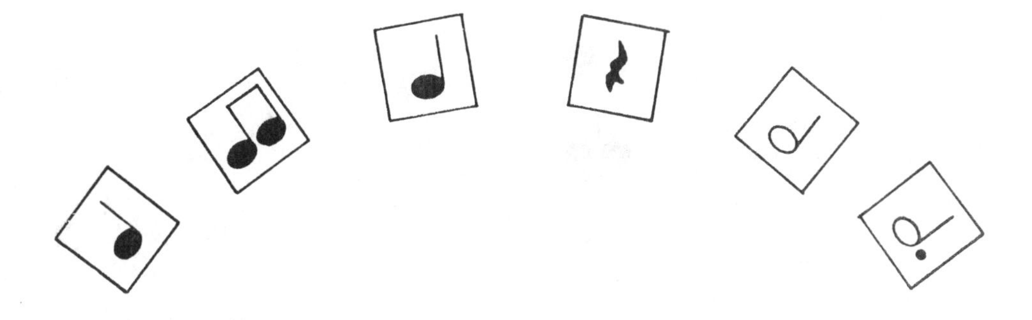

Starting with the card on the left, point to each card as you say the rhythm together. For ease, you may want to use a ruler as a pointer.

Next, clap and say the rhythm together.

Gather the cards and encourage the student to build another rainbow.

Have fun clapping and saying the rhythms for as long as the student is enjoying the activity. Remember, a successful learning experience ends on a positive note, not after the concentration and interest level has significantly dropped.

Roll And Identify I

PURPOSE: To have fun making the transition from the "fun names" to the true names of the notes and rest.

TEACHING AID: The note die

DIRECTIONS: Have the student roll the die and identify the note or rest which appears on top.

He will identify a quarter note as a "pink," for example. Explain that "pink" is your fun name for that note, but its true name is a quarter note. Have the student repeat the new term with you. Tell him the next time he rolls that note he can identify it as a quarter note rather than a pink note.

Introduce the real names for the remaining notes and the quarter rest as they appear. This game is a popular one. It helps to make the transition from the fun names to the true names almost effortless.

Begin to refer to the notes in the remaining activities in this Chapter by their real names for reinforcement. The notes and their real names are shown on the next page.

NOTE/REST	NAME OF NOTE/REST
♩	quarter note
♫	eighth notes
𝅗𝅥	half note
𝅗𝅥.	dotted-half note
𝅝	whole note
𝄽	quarter rest

Roll And Identify II

PURPOSE: To introduce the time values of quarter, eighth, half, dotted-half, and whole notes and the quarter rest.

TEACHING AID: The note die

DIRECTIONS: This activity is played in much the same way as "ROLL AND IDENTIFY I." Have the student roll the die and identify the note or rest appearing on top as a quarter note, half note, quarter rest, etc.

Each time a note appears tell the student how many counts that note receives. (He has already absorbed this information in a less specific manner through saying the "fun" names of the notes and in clapping them as well.)

Emphasize that, together, the two eighth notes equal one count--the same as the quarter note and quarter rest. The half note receives two counts, the whole note receives four counts, and the dotted-half note gets three (only older students can easily grasp the fact that a dot beside a note increases the time value of that note by one half of the note's value). Have the student roll the die, identifying the note or rest and how many counts it gets.

Challenge

PURPOSE: To have fun reviewing time values.

TEACHING AIDS: Approximately twenty rhythm cards

DIRECTIONS: Shuffle and deal the cards as you would playing cards.

Each player places his cards face down in a stack.

Both players simultaneously take the top card from their own stack and turn it over. Compare the time values. The player whose note has a greater time value wins both cards and places them face down on the bottom of his stack. For example, a dotted-half note will beat a quarter note as three counts are greater than one.

If the cards which are turned over are of equal value, then a "challenge" takes place. Each player turns over another card. The player whose note is of a greater time value wins all four cards. Any time a tie occurs continue turning over cards until the tie is broken.

The game continues in this manner until one player wins all of the cards.

Students especially enjoy this game and it is a fun way to reinforce time values.

Below is a list of time values:

♩	=	1 count
♫	=	1 count
𝄽	=	1 count
𝅗𝅥	=	2 counts
𝅗𝅥.	=	3 counts
𝅝	=	4 counts

More Rests

PURPOSE: To introduce half and whole rests and to review the quarter rest.

TEACHING AID: A pencil

DIRECTIONS: Point to the first rest on the staff shown on the next page. Say, "This is a whole rest and it gets four counts of silence."

As you point to the second rest explain that this is a half rest and gets two counts. Be sure that the student notices that the whole rest "hangs" from the fourth line and the half rest "sits" on the middle line.

"The third rest, as you know, is a quarter rest and receives one count."

Next, the student is to write the number of counts each rest receives on the lines provided below the staff. (Very young students may prefer to answer verbally.)

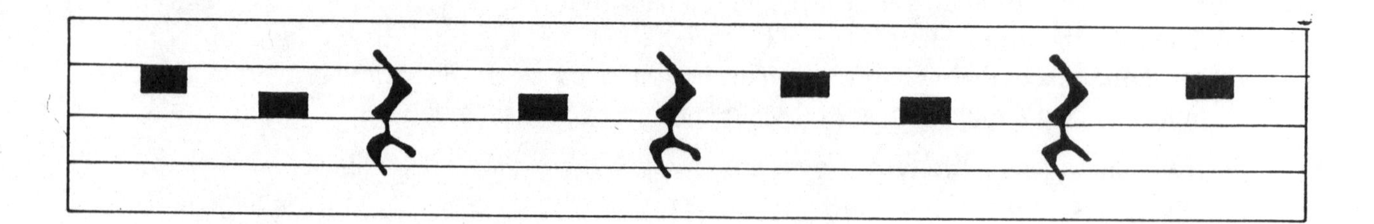

Are They Equal?

PURPOSE: To review and compare the time values of different notes and the quarter rest.

TEACHING AIDS: Rhythm cards (including quarter rests) - all colors

DIRECTIONS: Scatter the cards face up on the floor. Quickly review the time values of each note and the rest as you hold up the corresponding card.

Explain that you are going to choose a note and that you want the student to select a different type of note or a combination of notes which will equal the time value of the note you selected.

For example, choose a half note. The student is to choose a combination of different types of notes which will equal two counts.

Below are shown some of the possibilities:

Continue in the same manner as you and the student have fun discovering the many different combinations of notes which equal the same amount of counts.

On the next page is a sample of some of the combinations of notes which equal one another:

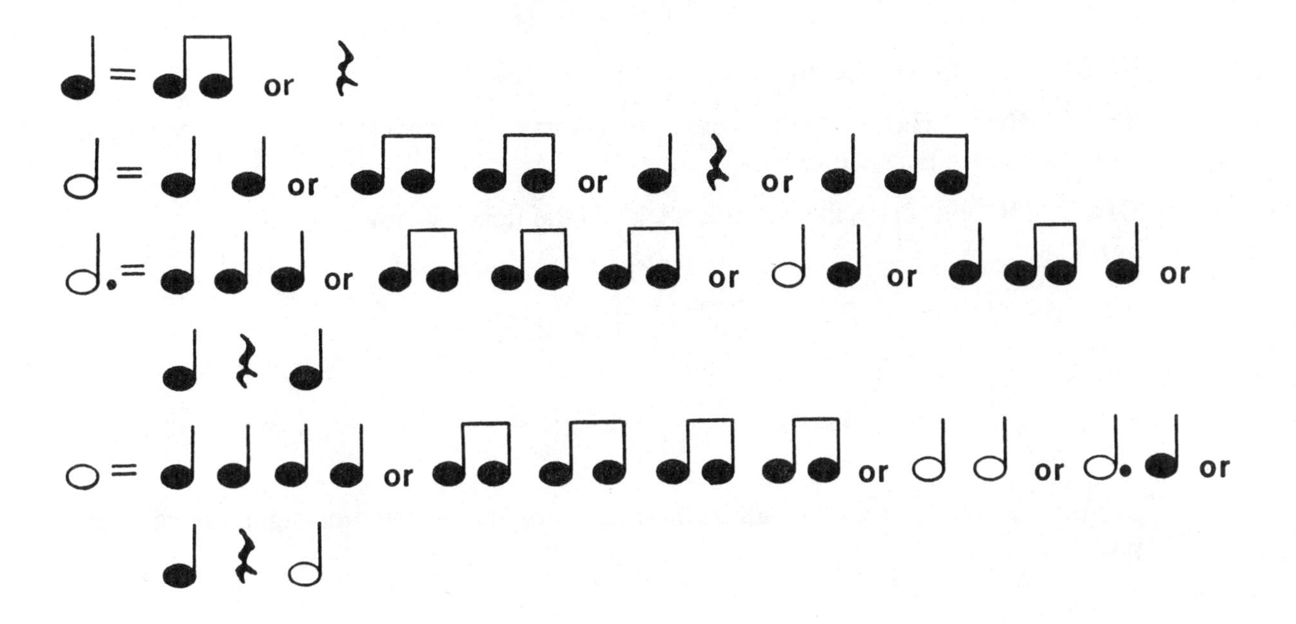

Time Signatures

PURPOSE: To introduce time signatures.

TEACHING AIDS: Time-signature cards and one of the student's piano books

2 4	3 4	4 4

DIRECTIONS: Place the time signature cards side by side on the floor.

"These are called time signatures and they provide us with very important information. The top number tells us how many counts are in each measure of the piece and the lower number tells us what type of note is to receive one count. For example, the two/four time signature tells us there will be two counts in every measure. The four represents a quarter note and reminds us that a quarter note will receive one count. The three/four time signature tells us there will be three counts in each measure and the four/four time signature signals four counts per measure."

Turn each card over to visually reinforce the fact that the four on the bottom represents a quarter note.

Next, look through the piano book with the student. Practice locating the time signature at the beginning of each piece. Have the student identify each time signature, telling you how many counts will be in each measure and what type of note will receive one count.

Skip over time signatures other than those introduced in this activity.

Add It Up

PURPOSE: To practice dividing rhythms into measures.

TEACHING AIDS: Rhythm cards (all colors), quarter-rest cards, time-signature cards, and three popsicle sticks

DIRECTIONS: Place the popsicle sticks on the floor as shown below:

Scatter the rhythm cards face up on the floor. Lay one of the time-signature cards in position.

3
4

Explain to the student that he is to place three counts in each measure. He may use any combination of notes which equal three counts.

A sample pattern is shown below:

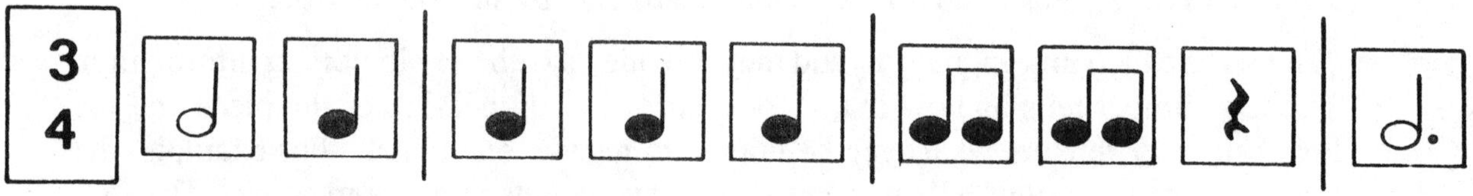

Point to the notes as, together, you and the student count aloud "one, two, three, one, two, three," etc., as shown below:

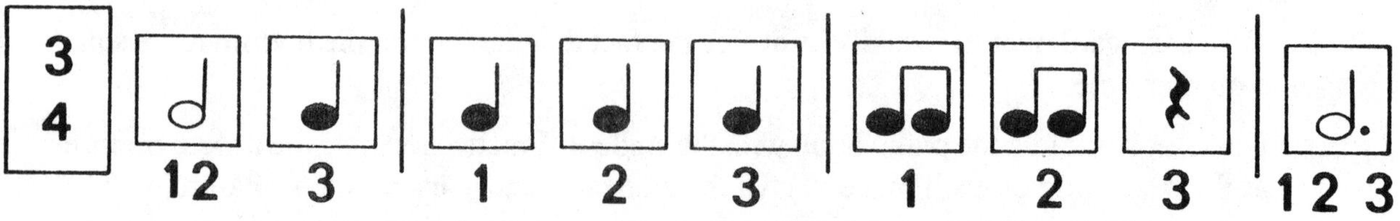

3
4

12 3 1 2 3 1 2 3 1 2 3

Remove the rhythm cards but keep the same time signature. Help the student to write another pattern using different combinations of notes.

Repeat the entire activity using the two/four and then the four/four time-signatures.

Other Time Signatures

PURPOSE: To review the two/four, three/four, and four/four time signatures and to introduce the three/eight and six/eight time signatures.

TEACHING AIDS: Time-signature cards

DIRECTIONS: Quickly review the two/four, three/four, and four/four time signatures.

Next, hold up the three/eight time signature card as you explain that, as always, the top number indicates how many counts per measure and the lower number represents the type of note which is to receive one count. An eight on the bottom indicates that an eighth note is to receive one count.

Turn the card over to visually reinforce this fact. (Explain, if necessary, that a single eighth note has a stem with a flag as the student is accustomed to seeing two eighth notes joined together.)

Next, hold up the six/eight time signature and have the student explain it to you.

NOTE: The three/eight and six/eight time signatures become more significant once they are introduced in the music. By that time, the student thoroughly understands the basic two/four, three/four, and four/four signatures and adapts to the concept of an eighth note receiving one count more readily.

To preview a student's first pieces in the newest time signatures, practice counting the pieces aloud together before the student begins to read the piece at the keyboard.

Shown below are the time values of various notes and rests based on an eighth note receiving one count.

♪ = (eighth note) = 1 count

𝄾 = (eighth rest) = 1 count

♩ = (quarter note) = 2 counts

𝄽 = (quarter rest) = 2 counts

♩. = (dotted-quarter note) = 3 counts

𝄽. = (dotted-quarter rest) = 3 counts

𝅗𝅥. = (dotted-half note) = 6 counts

Chapter V: INTERVALS

Intervals are a very important aspect of music theory. Whether melodic (successive notes) or harmonic (notes sounding simultaneously), intervals are an inherent part of music.

A beginning student can easily learn to identify half and whole steps at the keyboard and after he has mastered those skills found in Chapter I, he may be introduced to other intervals. Thirds are especially important as many of a student's earliest pieces are based on this interval. Much emphasis is placed on triads as well, which are chords built on thirds, otherwise known as tertian harmony. After becoming acquainted with intervals at the keyboard, the student will practice associating them with their placement on the staff.

Half Steps

PURPOSE: To introduce the student to half steps at the keyboard.

TEACHING AID: A piano

DIRECTIONS: Stand at the keyboard with the student.

Explain that a half step is the distance between any key and its nearest neighbor, either higher or lower.

Play any C, then play the neighboring C# (the black note one half step higher). "Can you find another C on the keyboard and locate the note a half step higher?" (The terms sharp and flat need not be mentioned yet.)

Practice locating half steps all over the keyboard, both higher and lower than the original key, which should be sometimes white and sometimes black. Remember to locate the half steps between B and C and E and F as these are the only half steps which occur between white keys.

NOTE: To introduce the terms sharp and flat and to reinforce the concept of half steps, cover "ACCIDENTALS" found in Chapter VII before going on to "WHOLE STEPS," where you can review these new terms.

Fun Page - Half Steps

PURPOSE: To reinforce the concept of half steps.

TEACHING AIDS: Crayons

DIRECTIONS: Have the student use a red crayon to color the keys which are a half step higher than the keys marked with an X.

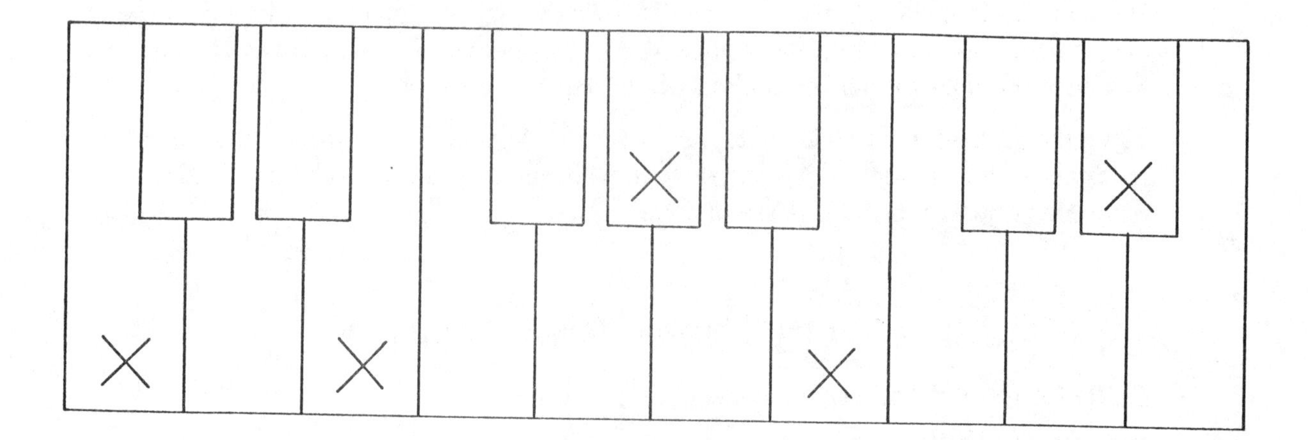

Using a blue crayon, the student is to color the keys (shown on the next page) which are a half step lower than the keys marked with an X.

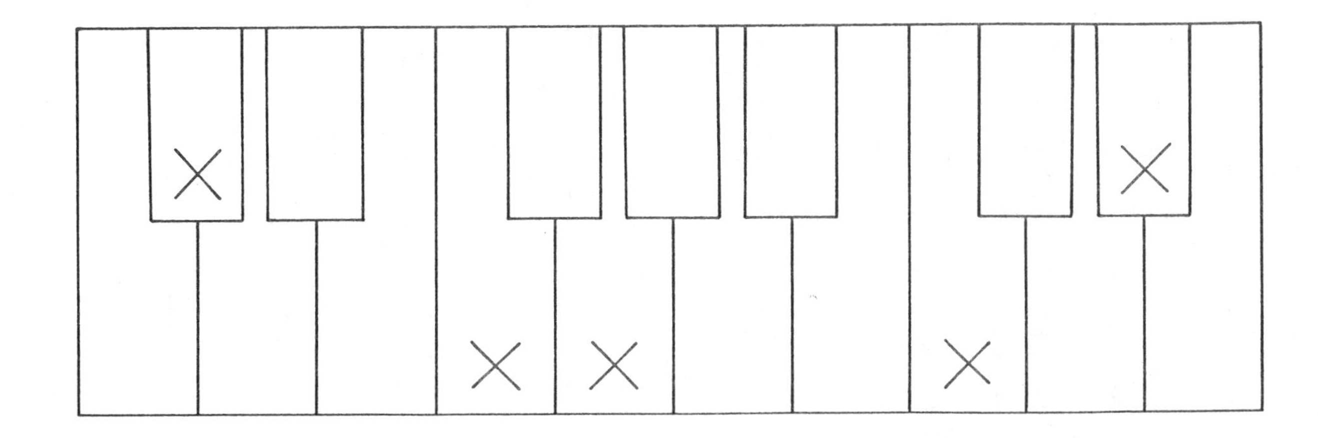

Whole Steps

PURPOSE: To introduce the student to whole steps at the keyboard.

TEACHING AIDS: A piano and several pennies

DIRECTIONS: First, take a minute to review half steps at the keyboard.

"As you know, a half step is the distance between any key and its nearest neighbor either higher or lower. Today, I want to introduce you to whole steps. A whole step consists of two consecutive half steps." Demonstrate this concept at the keyboard. Play a C and then play the D which is a whole step higher. Double check by locating the half step between C and C# and the other half step between C# and D.

Have the student play another C and locate the key a whole step higher. Practice double checking the number of half steps and also point out that there will always be just one key between the original key and its whole step neighbor.

Have the student locate whole steps all over the keyboard. Be sure to introduce him to some of the "trickier" whole steps such as Eb up to F and C down to Bb as well as examples in which both keys are black.

Fun Page - Whole Steps

PURPOSE: To reinforce the concept of whole steps.

TEACHING AIDS: Crayons

DIRECTIONS: Have the student use a green crayon to color the keys which are a whole step higher than the keys marked with an X in the illustration on the next page.

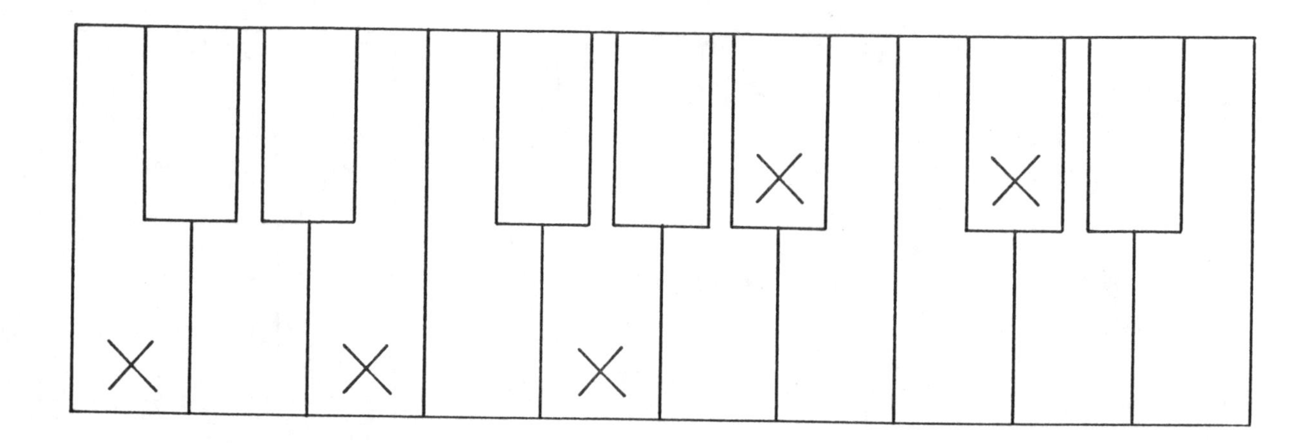

Using an orange crayon, the student is to color the keys that are a whole step lower than the keys marked with an X.

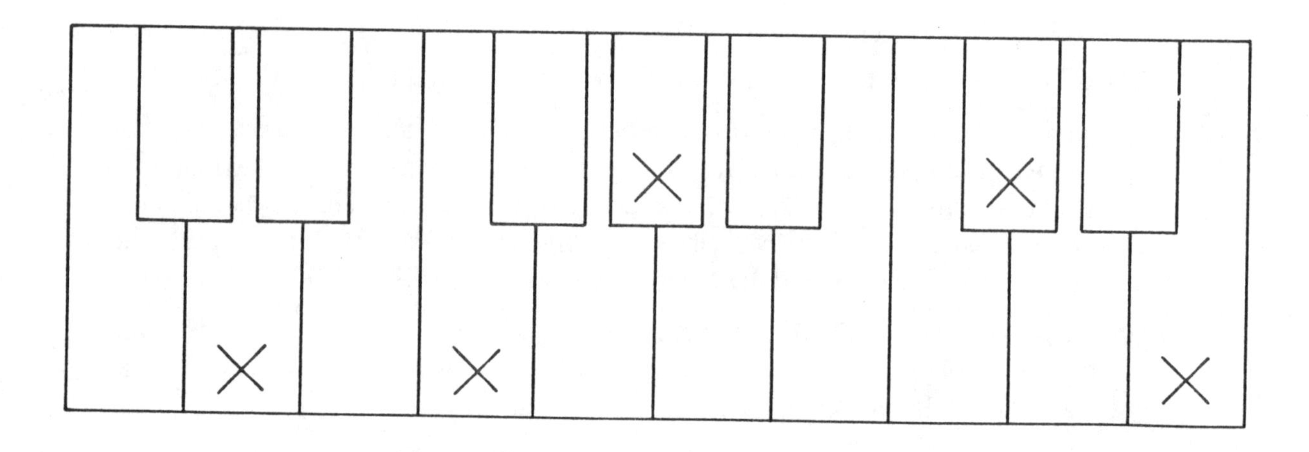

Seconds And Thirds

PURPOSE: To help the student differentiate between seconds and thirds.

TEACHING AIDS: Two sets of alphabet cards

DIRECTIONS: Sit on the floor beside the student.
Lay the cards on the floor as shown on the next page. Set the others aside.

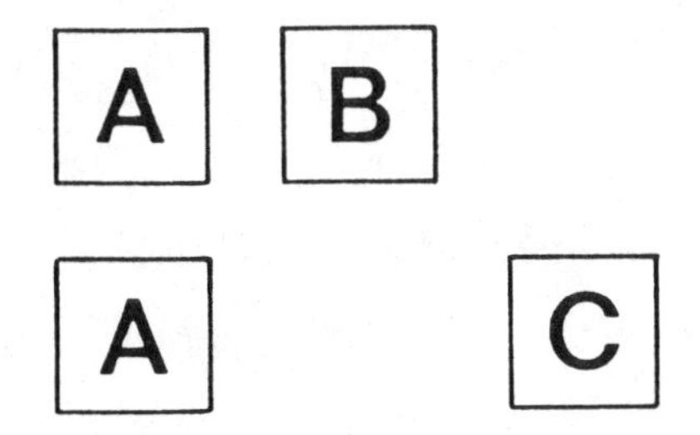

"Today we are going to talk about intervals of a second and of a third. An interval is the distance in pitch between two notes."

Point to the A and B in the top row as you explain that to go "next door" is to move an interval of a second, but when you skip over a note as you do when you move from A to C (point to those cards) you are moving an interval of a third.

Gather those cards and replace them with the ones shown below:

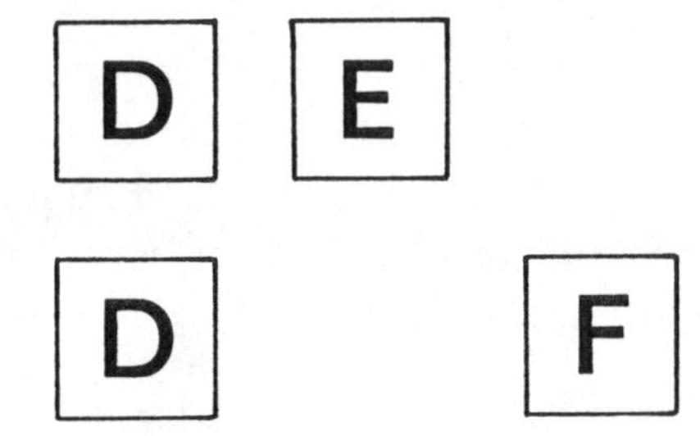

Point to the top row as you ask, "If I go from D to neighboring E, am I moving an internal of a second or a third? Right, that is a second. Now tell me whether the interval from D to F (point to those cards) is a second or a third. Yes, to skip from D up to F is a third."

If necessary, repeat the above step once more using E and F on the top row and E and G on the bottom.

Finally, arrange some of the cards in groups of two in front of the student as shown below. Some of the groups will represent seconds and the others thirds. Have the student tell you whether the letters in each group are "next door neighbors" or whether they are a skip apart and then identify the interval as a second or a third.

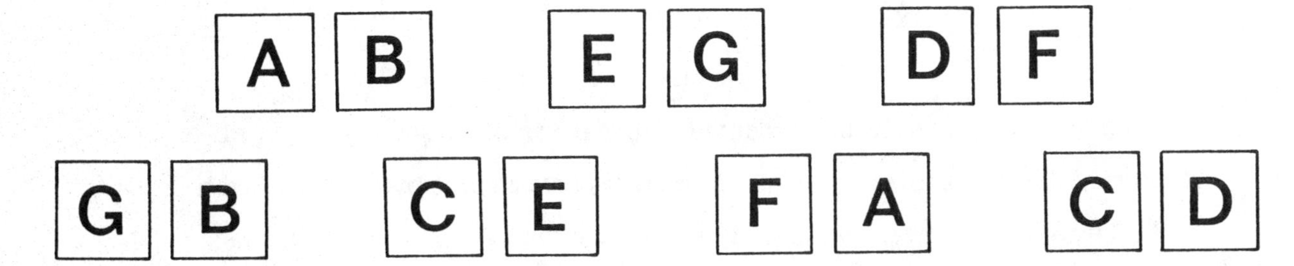

Repeat this step several times until the student identifies the intervals with ease.

Seconds And Thirds On The Staff

PURPOSE: To help the student differentiate between seconds and thirds on the staff.

TEACHING AIDS: A one-staff board and plain notes

DIRECTIONS: Place the notes on the staff as shown below:

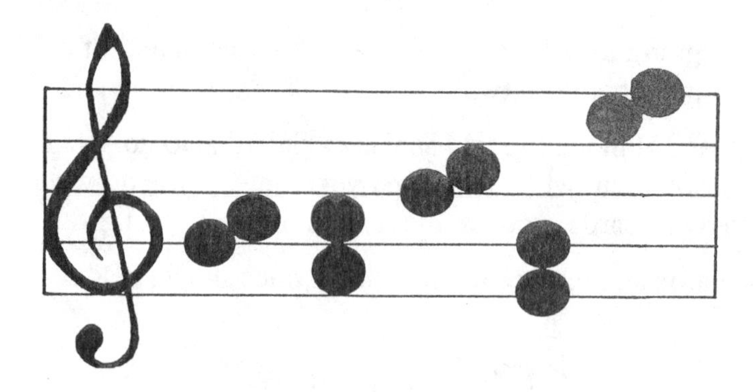

"Seconds are very easy to spot on the staff; they appear to be riding piggyback style." Point to the first, third and fifth groups of notes.

"Thirds, as you know, are a skip apart. This means that the notes in any series of thirds will either be all line notes or all space notes."

Check the thirds on the staff to confirm this fact.

Remove the notes and rearrange them as shown below:

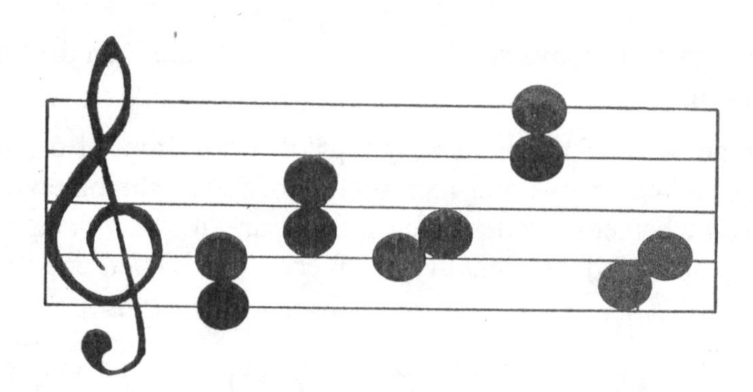

Point to each interval as the student identifies it as either a second or a third.

Repeat this step until the student differentiates between the two intervals with ease.

Finally, place the notes on the staff in a melodic manner as shown on the next page:

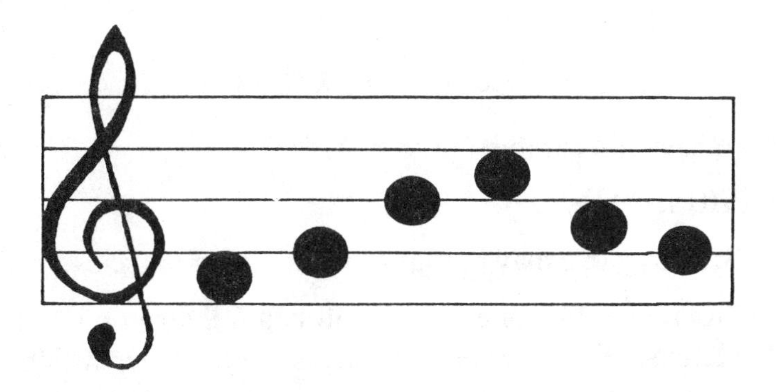

Help the student to name the interval between each of the notes. For example, the interval between the first and second notes is a second. The interval between the second and third notes is a third, etc.

Initially, it may be more difficult for the student to identify the melodic intervals as opposed to the harmonic intervals. Repeat this last step many times. Vary the melody slightly each time using only seconds and thirds and limit the pattern to six or seven notes.

Got'cha

PURPOSE: To have fun spelling thirds.

TEACHING AIDS: One set of alphabet cards and a GOT'CHA card of the same size and color

DIRECTIONS: Place the A face up on the floor. Scatter the other cards, including the GOT'CHA card, face down.

"What letter is a skip above A? Right, C. Turn over the alphabet cards one at a time until you locate C. If you turn over an alphabet card other than the one you need, simply return the card face down. When you find C, take that card and place it to the right of A. I hope you manage to avoid the GOT'CHA card; if you turn over that card, we have to start the game all over again! Now, let's see how lucky you are today."

Each time a third is added say them aloud together starting with A.

As the game continues the student will become aware of the value of memorizing the placement of the cards which are returned face down.

When the GOT'CHA card is turned over, gather all the cards and shuffle them. Place A on the floor as before and turn the remaining cards face down to prepare to start again.

The game is over when the student successfully avoids the GOT'CHA card while positioning all of the thirds in the correct order.

The next time you play, choose a different letter to begin the game.

Rotation Thirds

PURPOSE: To have fun naming thirds verbally.

TEACHING AIDS: None

DIRECTIONS: This game may be played while riding in the car, waiting in line, etc.

Explain that in rotation thirds one of you will begin the game by naming one of the music alphabet letters. The other player must name the letter which is a third higher. The turns continue to rotate in this manner until you return to the original letter, such as B...D...F...A...C...E...G...B.

Practice starting with a different letter in each round and occasionally say the intervals in descending (backward) order.

More Thirds

PURPOSE: To gain ease in thinking thirds forward and backward.

TEACHING AIDS: Several buttons (or Cheerios which are fun to eat afterward) and a piano

DIRECTIONS: Stand at the keyboard with the student.

Ask the student to choose any white key in the middle register, identify it and place a button on it. Have him name several thirds to the right of that key, placing a button on each key as he identifies it.

Remove all the buttons and again have the student select a key, identify it and place a button on it. Have him name several thirds to the left of this key, again placing a button on each third as he names the key.

Thinking the alphabet backward is challenging for young students but is a skill which every developing pianist must master.

Spelling Triads

PURPOSE: To introduce triads.

TEACHING AIDS: Three sets of alphabet cards

DIRECTIONS: Sit on the floor beside the student.

"We have practiced spelling thirds several times recently so I know you will find it easy to spell triads. A triad is simply a three-note chord built on thirds."

Lay an A on the floor. "What note is a third above A? Right, C." Place a C to the right of A. "Now, a third above C is.....yes, E." Position an E next to C. "See how easy it is to build a triad?"

Practice building other triads.

Finally, divide the cards into seven groups of three cards each which spell triads. Lay the cards on the floor in a manner which is like or similar to the illustration shown below. The student is to identify the cards which are face down before turning them over to verify his answer.

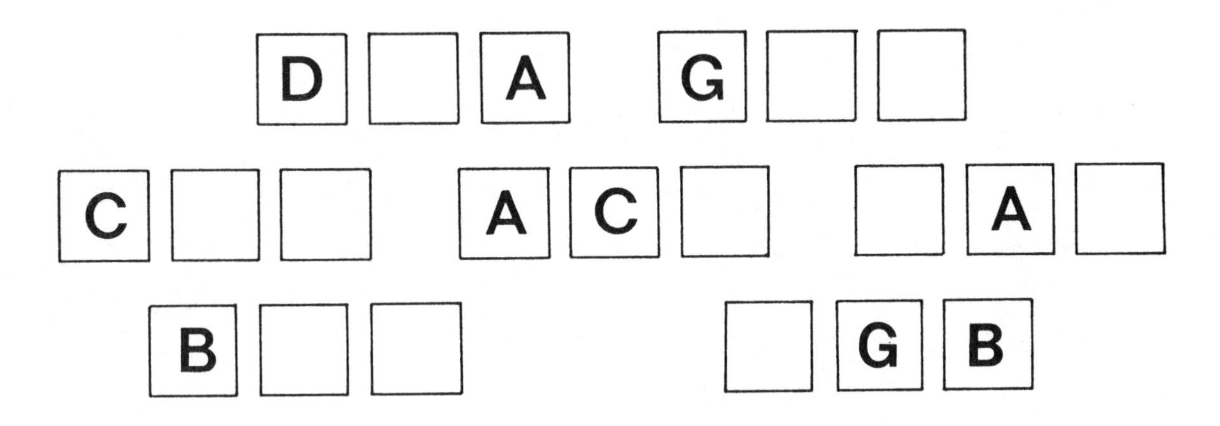

Fun Page - Triad Caterpillars

PURPOSE: To practice spelling triads.

TEACHING AID: A pencil

DIRECTIONS: The student is to fill in the blanks so that each caterpillar spells a triad.

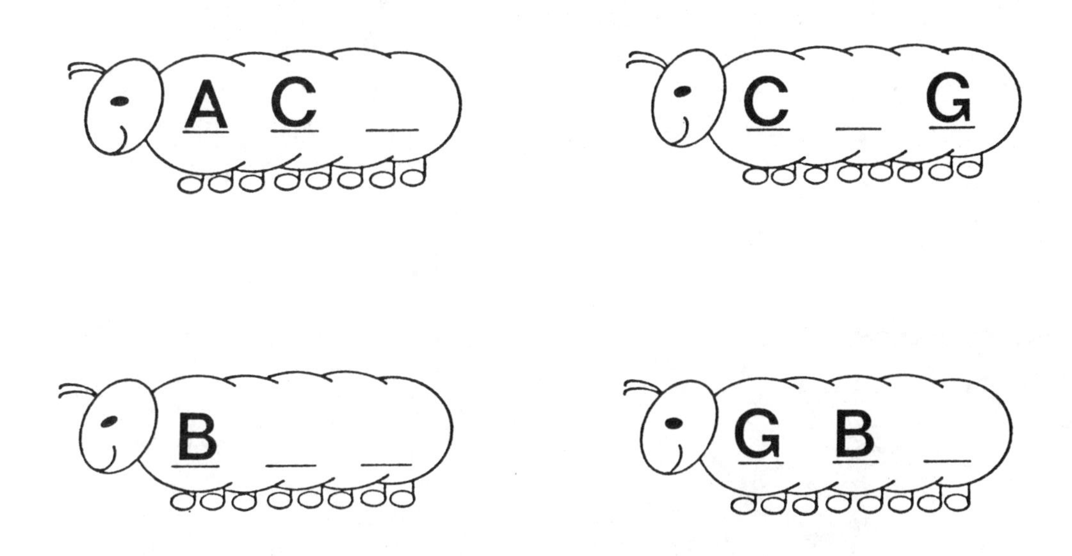

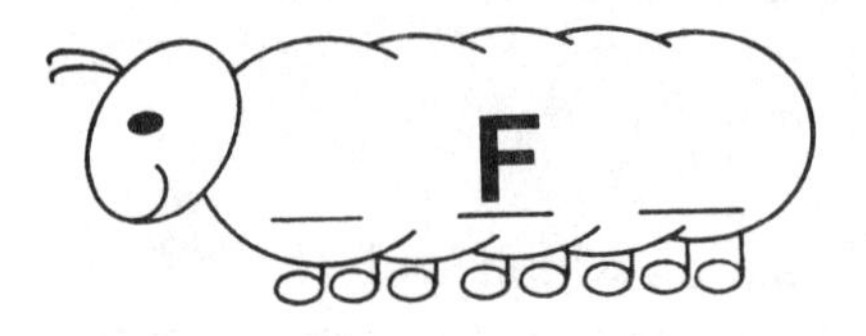

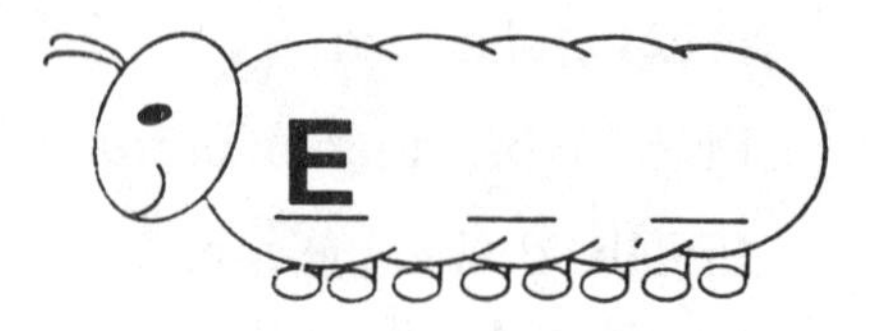

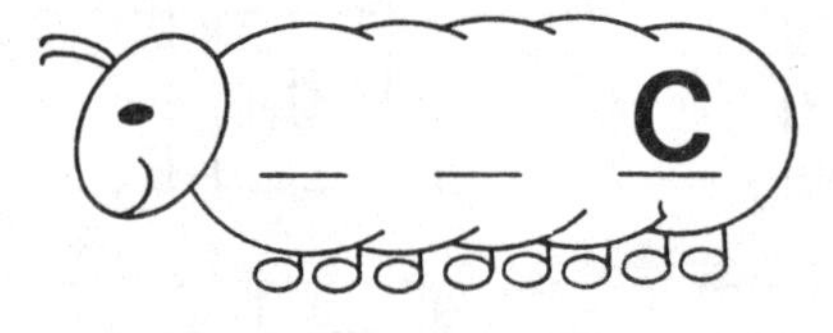

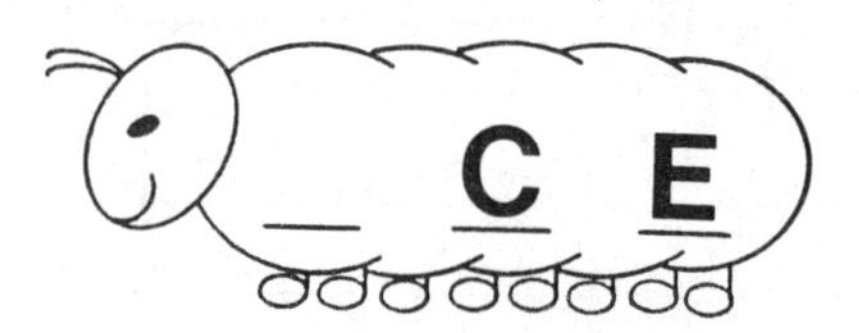

_ D _

_ B D

D _ A

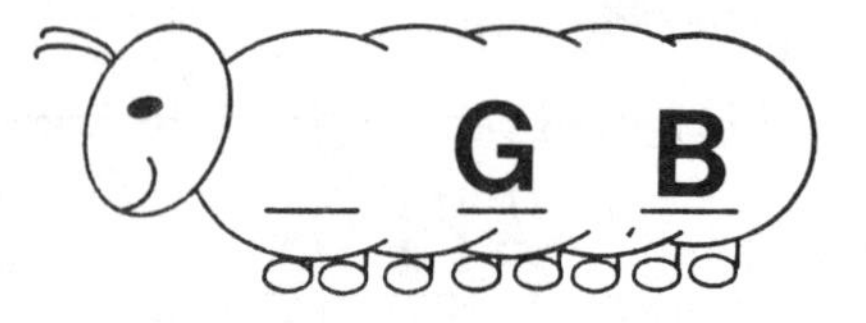

Seconds And Other Intervals

PURPOSE: To review seconds and thirds and to introduce fourths through octaves.

TEACHING AIDS: Two sets of alphabet cards

DIRECTIONS: Sit on the floor beside the student.

Place an A in front of the student. Add a B to the right of A.

For review ask the student, "If the interval between A up to B is a second, what is the interval between A up to C?" (Exchange the B with a C as you ask.) "Yes, that is be a third."

Replace the C with a D. The student should identify that interval as a fourth.

Continue in the same manner. When the student has identified the interval from C up to B as a seventh, replace the B with a C.

"Now we have stepped up once more and you notice the letters are the same. The word used to define the distance of eight pitches is an octave."

The student will enjoy adding this term to his music vocabulary.

Next, collect the cards and lay any two cards on the floor side by side. Help the student to identify the interval.

Continue laying down the remaining cards in groups of two as the student names each interval.

Win an Interval

PURPOSE: To practice identifying intervals.

TEACHING AIDS: Two sets of alphabet cards

DIRECTIONS: Sit on the floor facing the student. Hold the cards as you would a hand of playing cards. Have the student select one card and place it face up on the floor. Instruct the student to select a second card and place it to the right of the first.

If, for example, the two cards selected by the student are C and E, he should identify the interval from C up to E. If he correctly identifies the interval as a third, he wins and keeps the first card (C); the E will remain on the floor to become the lower letter of the next interval. Should the student make an incorrect identification, gently correct his error, place the card representing the higher letter of the interval back into your hand and encourage the student to choose again.

Play until the student wins all of the cards in your hand.

Race to The Top

PURPOSE: To introduce the concept that to move stepwise on the staff one moves by seconds and that the distance between the bass and treble staves is measured by seconds as well.

TEACHING AIDS: A two-staff board, two plain notes, a popsicle stick, a small paper bag and several slips of paper on which are written directions such as "up a second," "down a third," "up a fourth," etc. (Use all of the intervals up to and including the octave.)

DIRECTIONS: Place the popsicle stick on the staff to represent middle C. Put both notes on the lowest line of the bass staff and place the slips of paper in the paper bag.

The youngest player goes first by reaching into the bag and removing one slip of paper. It might read, for example, "up a third," in which case the player will move his note up to the next line of the bass clef. To do this in a manner which will help the student to identify intervals on the staff with ease, have the student say "one" to indicate the lowest line (the starting point), "two," as he moves his note to the space, and "three" as he places the note on the next line. Each player should count in this manner throughout the game. To continue, the slip of paper is returned to the bag and the turn rotates to the other player(s).

If a player selects a slip of paper directing him to move a number of steps which would cause him to move below the lowest line or above the highest line, then that slip of paper is returned to the bag and the player does not move his note at all.

Remember that there is only one line (and therefore two spaces) between the staves, which are separated on the music page only for visual clarity.

The goal of each player is to reach the top line of the treble staff first; however, the winner must land on that line exactly. For instance, if a player who is a second away from the top line draws a slip of paper which reads "up a third," that player cannot move. He must wait to draw the paper which reads "up a second."

Children enjoy playing this game which is a good pre-reading activity.

Chapter VI: NOTE IDENTIFICATION

At first, the student will learn the names of the notes on the staff by concentrating on just the line notes or just the space notes, therefore, he needs to be thoroughly familiar with thirds which are introduced in Chapter V.

Soon, however, the student will be naming all of the notes on the staff. He will be introduced to the ledger line notes and will begin working with staff cards. Frequent (preferably daily) review is necessary for the thorough memorization of the notes; this is why there are so many activities in this Chapter which focus on review. The fun pages provide reinforcement as well.

Although the activities are written for the treble staff, the same activities may be used, with a minimum of adjustment, to teach the bass clef notes when the student is ready.

Just Lines

PURPOSE: To practice naming the line notes on the treble staff.

TEACHING AIDS: A one-staff board and notes with names

DIRECTIONS: Sit on the floor beside the student facing the staff board.

Point to the treble clef as you explain, "The treble clef is also known as the G clef because its position on the staff determines which line is G. As you can see, the clef curls around the second line, which indicates that that line is G. If I could move the clef so that it curled around the top line, then that line would be G. In piano music, though, the second line will always be G and the clef will be in the position that you see now."

Place the G note in position.

To emphasize the note on the lowest line, place the E on that line as you say with a twinkle in your eye, "See how e-e-e-easy it is to remember this note?"

Finally, help the student to determine the names of the remaining lines and to place the notes in position.

The staff board should look like this:

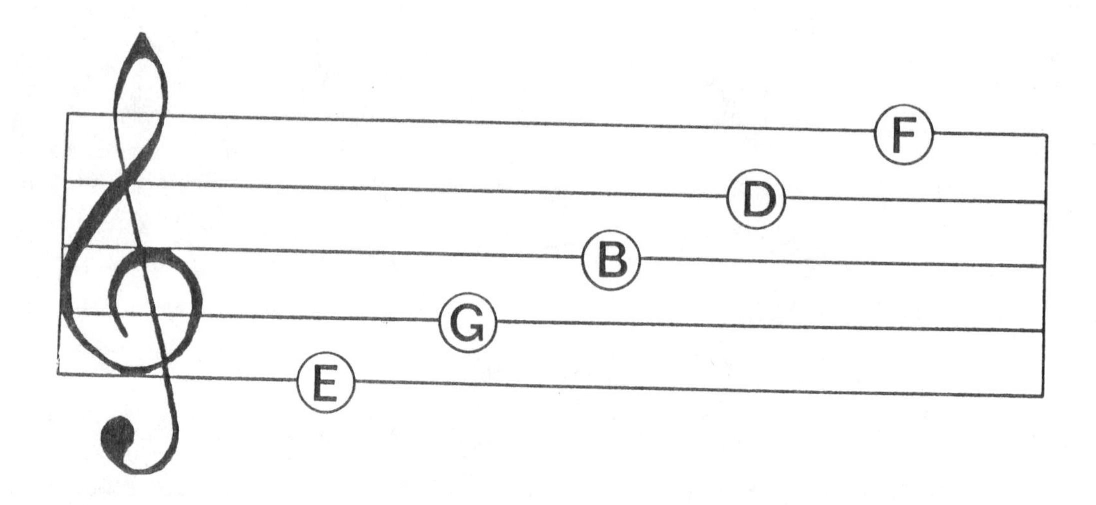

Point to each note as you say together, "E...G...B...D...F." Do this several times.

Remove the notes and ask the student to place them in order on the staff. Reinforce the fun association with E and the relationship of G to the treble clef.

Just Spaces

PURPOSE: To introduce the space notes on the treble staff.

TEACHING AIDS: A one-staff board and notes with names

DIRECTIONS: Place the notes on the staff as shown below:

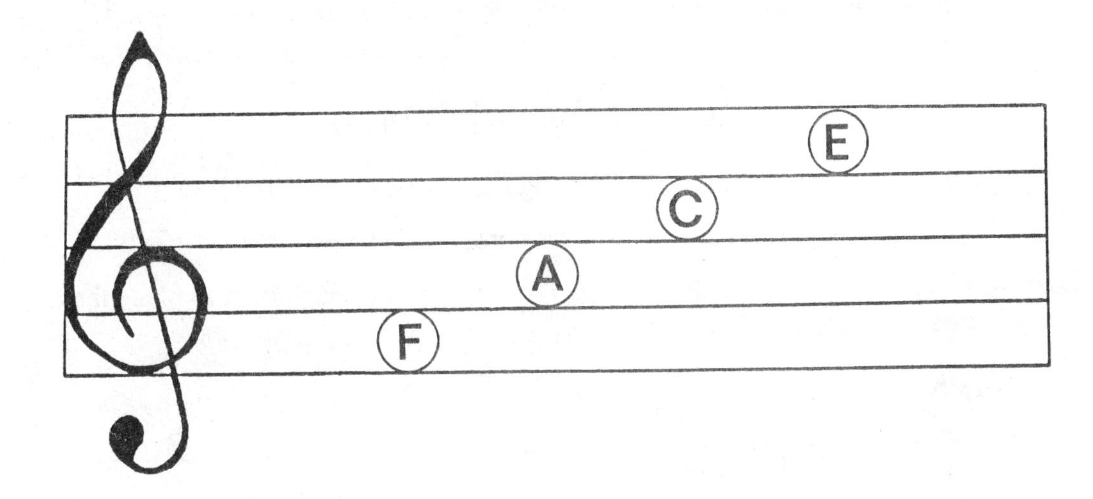

Say together the names of the notes several times, starting with F.

Next, turn each note face down. Point to the lowest note and ask the student to identify it. Have him turn the note over to confirm his answer. If he answers incorrectly, have him return the note face down and come back to that note later.

Continue in the same manner with the remaining notes. At first, have the student identify the notes in order, but quickly begin to skip around for a more challenging activity.

Sad Cecil

PURPOSE: To have fun reviewing the notes on the treble staff.

TEACHING AIDS: A one-staff board, notes with names (all of the same color) and Sad Cecil (same color and size as the notes)

NOTE: At first, use this activity to review just the space notes or just the line notes. Later, review all of the notes at the same time.

DIRECTIONS: Place the staff board on the floor. Have the student close his eyes as you scatter the notes and Sad Cecil face down around the staff board.

The student is to turn over the notes one by one and place them in the appropriate positions on the staff. Hopefully, he can complete this task before selecting Sad Cecil. Each time Sad Cecil is chosen, and after the moans and groans have ceased, have the student close his eyes as you remove any notes on the staff and rearrange them (including Sad Cecil) face down on the floor in order to begin again.

The game continues until the student successfully positions all of the notes on the staff while avoiding Sad Cecil.

Students love to play this game again and again. Be sure they have mastered the names of the lines and spaces before proceeding to the next activity.

Lines And Spaces Together

PURPOSE: To practice identifying line and space notes on the treble staff.

TEACHING AIDS: A one-staff board and notes with names

DIRECTIONS: Place the staff board on the floor. Help the student to place the line notes in position as shown below:

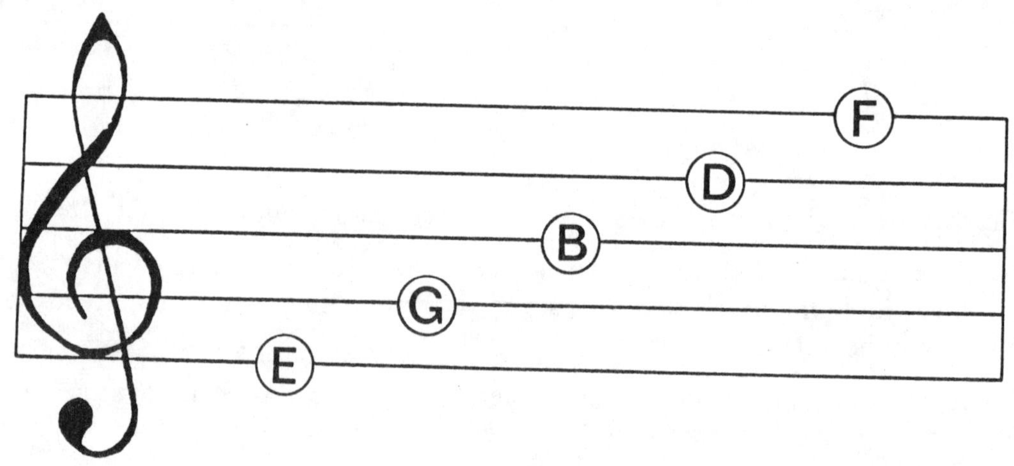

"What letter comes between E and G? Right, F." Have the student place the F note in position.

Continue in this manner to fill the remaining three spaces as shown below:

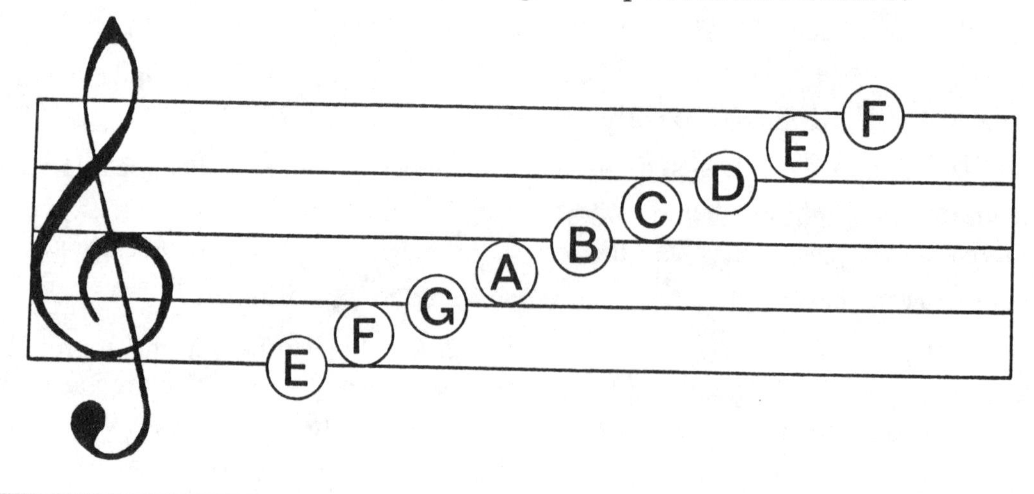

Finally, explain that you want to introduce two new notes. Place a D below E and a G above F.

The finished staff board should look like this:

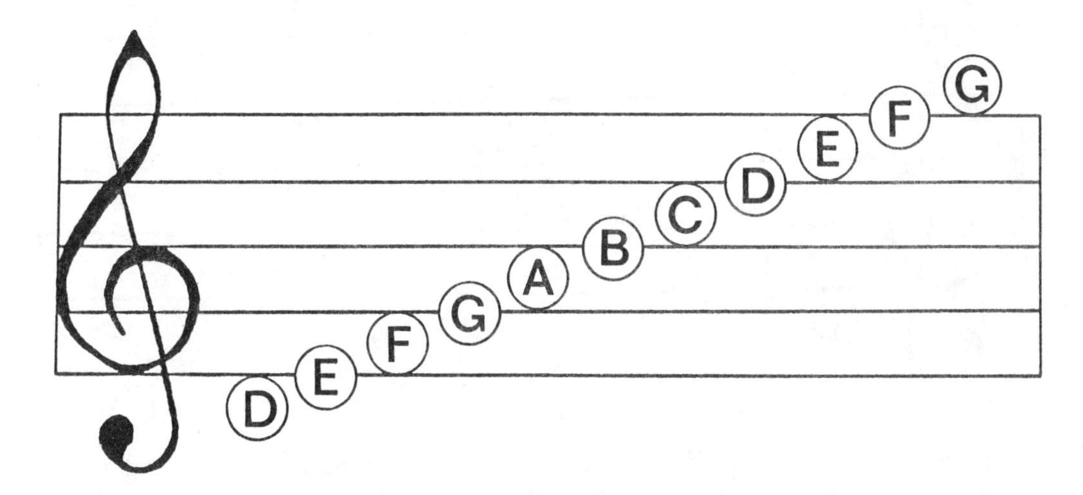

Starting with D, point to each note as, together, you and the student say the letter names aloud.

Remove the notes from the staff. Challenge the student to put the notes back on the staff in their proper positions. Encourage him to start with the lowest note and work his way to the top in order.

Gently guide the student to the appropriate line or space when necessary and be sure to offer enthusiastic praise as he accomplishes his task.

NOTE: The next time the student plays "Sad Cecil" using just space notes, remember to include the two newest notes--D and G.

Connecting The Staff To The Keyboard

PURPOSE: To review the notes on the treble staff and to begin to associate their placement on the staff to their position on the keyboard.

TEACHING AIDS: A one-staff board, notes with names, and a piano

DIRECTIONS: Stand at the keyboard with the student.

Place the piano bench with the staff board resting on top of it slightly under the keyboard so that the student can play keys in the middle register and look down at the staff board for reference.

Have the student place the notes in order on the staff starting with D as shown below:

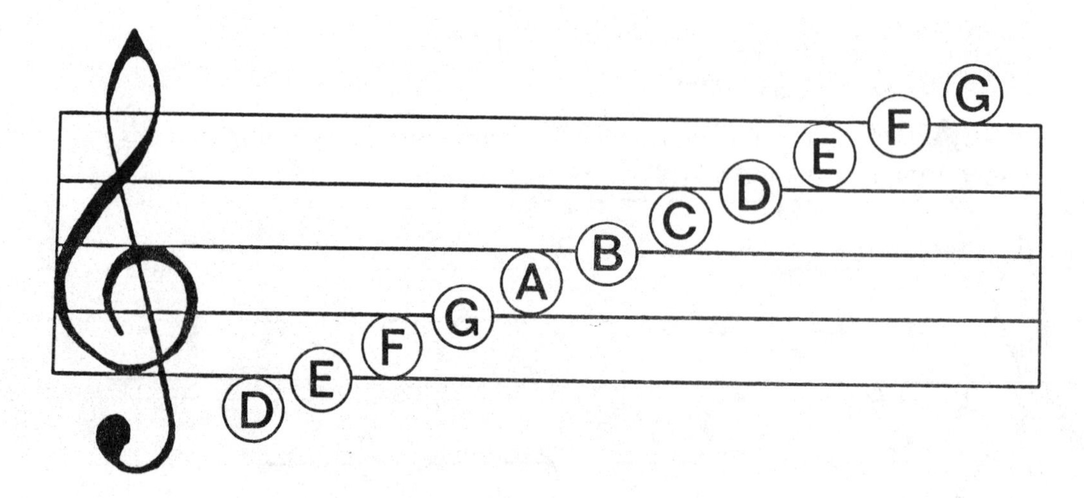

Explain to the student that each line and space on the staff refers to one particular key. For example, while there are several D's on the keyboard, the lowest D on the treble staff (point to that note) refers only to the one near the center of the keyboard. Play the corresponding key as you point out that this D is easy to locate because it is just below the name of the piano.

Point to the neighboring E on the staff as you play the matching key. "As the notes step higher on the staff, they step higher on the keyboard also."

Let the student play the remaining keys one at a time as you point to the notes in order. Say the letter names aloud together.

When you are finished go back and point to the lowest note again. Check to see if the student remembers where that D is found on the piano.

Reviewing The Lines And Spaces

PURPOSE: To review the names of the lines and spaces of the treble staff.

TEACHING AIDS: One set of alphabet cards plus an extra D, E, F, and G, notes with names, and a one-staff board

DIRECTIONS: Place the staff board on the floor and scatter the notes face up around the board. Hold the cards as you would a hand of playing cards. Instruct the student to select an alphabet card, locate the matching note and place it on the appropriate line or space.

Some of the letters are found in two different positions on the staff. Encourage the student to find both positions and avoid placing more than one note on any given line or space.

Fun Page - Note Identification

PURPOSE: To identify notes on the treble staff.

TEACHING AID: A pencil

DIRECTIONS: The student is to identify each note. (Very young students may prefer to identify the notes verbally.)

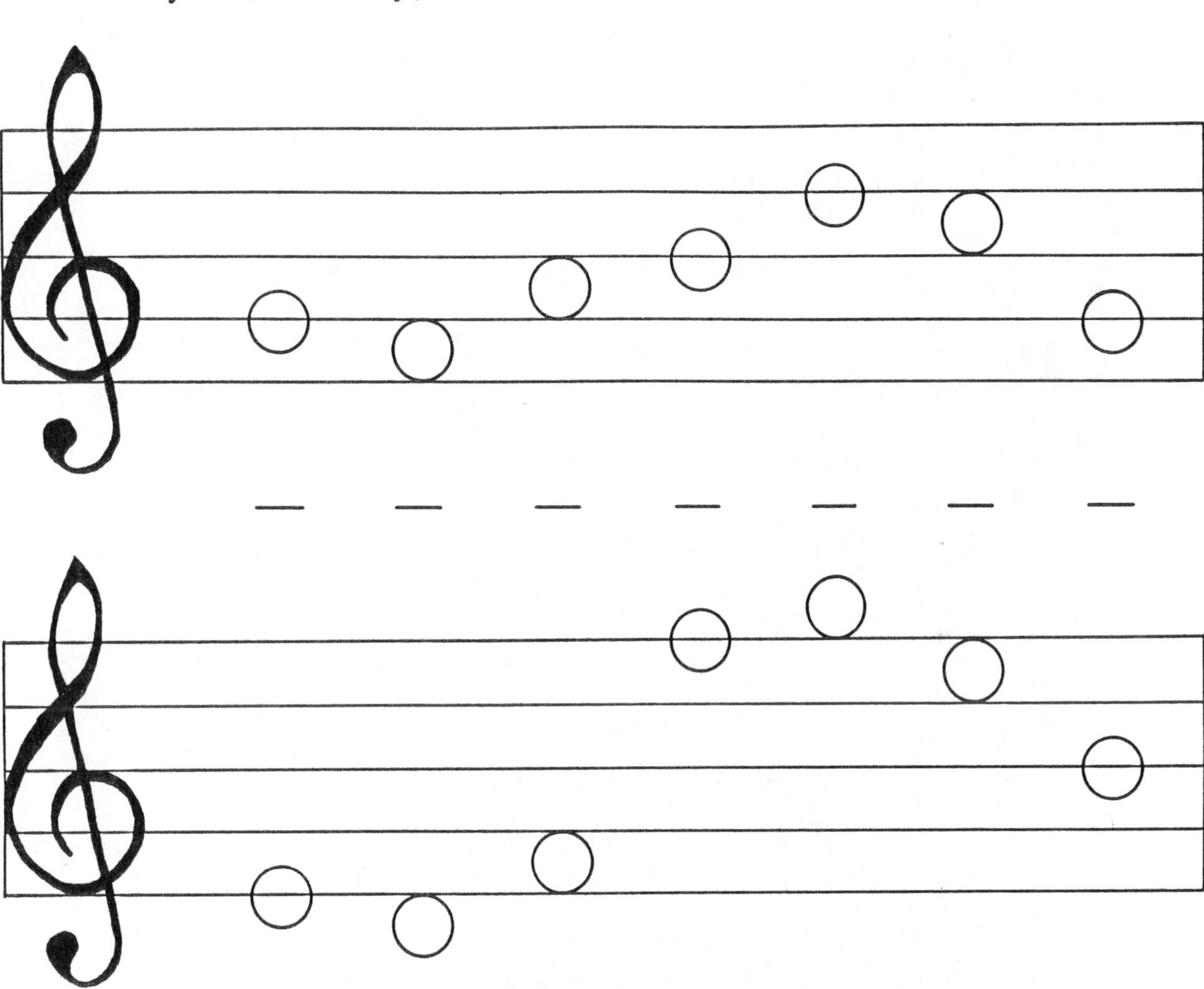

Draw It

PURPOSE: To reinforce the names of the lines and spaces of the treble staff and to practice drawing notes on the staff.

TEACHING AIDS: One set of alphabet cards and a pencil

DIRECTIONS: Hold the alphabet cards as you would a hand of playing cards. Have the student choose a card and draw a whole note (a circle with no stem) on the corresponding line or space.

If necessary, guide the student to the appropriate answer on the staff.

Continue in the same manner with the remaining alphabet cards.

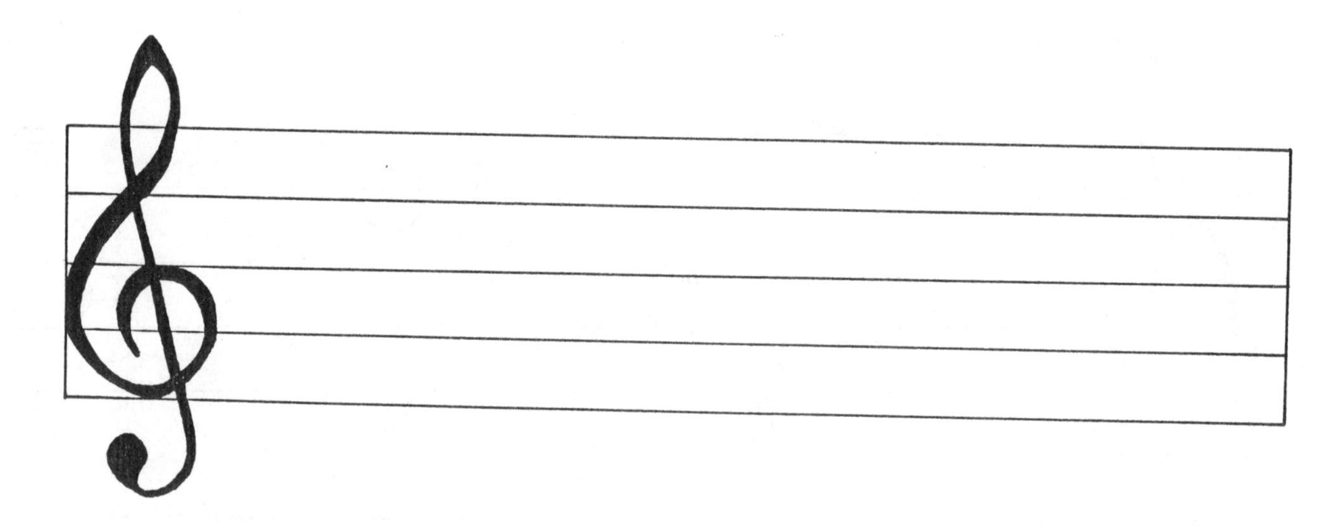

Introducing Staff Cards

PURPOSE: To introduce staff cards and to practice naming the notes on the treble staff.

TEACHING AIDS: A one-staff board, notes with names, and staff cards

DIRECTIONS: Sit on the floor with the student facing the staff board.

Help the student to place the notes in position on the staff.

Next, show the student a staff card as you encourage him to identify the note by using the notes on the staff board as a visual reference.

Continue in the same manner with the remaining staff cards.

Matches

PURPOSE: To practice identifying notes on the staff.

TEACHING AIDS: Several staff cards and matching alphabet cards

DIRECTIONS: Choose three or four staff cards and lay them face up and side by side on the floor. Hold the matching alphabet cards as you would a hand of playing cards. Have the student select the alphabet cards one at a time and place each one on top of the corresponding staff card.

Gently guide the student to the appropriate card when necessary.

Repeat the activity using different staff cards and the matching alphabet cards.

To make the game more challenging, include extra alphabet cards in your hand. Now, a chosen alphabet card will not necessarily match any of the staff cards.

Should the student determine he has selected one of the extra alphabet cards, simply ask him to lay it aside until the end of that round.

Finally, for students who are spelling and recognizing simple words, arrange the staff cards so that they spell different words. The student will delight in discovering the words as he reinforces the names of the notes.

Slap Down

PURPOSE: To have fun naming treble staff notes using staff cards.

TEACHING AIDS: Approximately eleven staff cards and two sets of alphabet cards

DIRECTIONS: Sit on the floor facing the student. Each of you receives a set of alphabet cards which should be arranged face up on the floor for easy reference.

Shuffle the staff cards and place them in a stack face down on the floor between you and the student.

Take the top staff card and turn it over. Both you and the student should quickly and silently identify the note, scan your alphabet cards and slap the appropriate card on top of the staff card. The player who slaps down the correct answer first wins, and keeps the staff card and then places his alphabet card back into position.

Next, the student will take his turn and turn over the next staff card. The game continues as before until all of the staff cards have been identified and won.

Note Spell

PURPOSE: To have fun reviewing the notes on the treble staff.

TEACHING AIDS: A one-staff board and plain notes

NOTE: This activity is recommended for students who can read simple words.

DIRECTIONS: Sit on the floor beside the student facing the staff board. Place three notes on the staff so that they spell the word bag.

"If you read these notes from left to right you will find that they spell a word. Can you tell me what it is?" (Point to each note as the student identifies it to insure that he is reading them in the proper order.)

"Right, these notes spell the word bag. Let's try another."

Spell longer and more difficult words according to the student's capabilities.

Listed below are some sample words. Also refer to "SPELL IT" for more terms.

beg	fad	age
cad	edge	cabbage
bad	bead	baggage

Spell It

PURPOSE: To have fun reviewing the notes on the treble staff.

TEACHING AIDS: A one-staff board, notes with names, slips of paper on which a word is written which can be spelled on the staff, and a small paper bag

NOTE: This game is designed for students who can read simple words.

DIRECTIONS: Sit on the floor with the student facing the staff board.

Place the slips of paper in the paper bag. Have the student reach in, pull out one slip of paper and using the notes, spell that word on the staff.

Help the student to position the notes correctly so that one reads the notes from left to right.

Some sample words are listed below:

bag	deaf	egg	cab
add	badge	fed	ace
dad	bed	cage	face

Naming Ledger Line Notes I

PURPOSE: To practice naming the ledger line notes above and below the treble staff.

TEACHING AIDS: A one-staff board, four popsicle sticks, and notes with names

DIRECTIONS: Place the sticks in position as shown on the next page:

Place a C on the lowest ledger line so that the line (or stick) seem to run through the center of the note. "This ledger line note is known as middle C as it is the C nearest the center of the keyboard." (If a piano is nearby, help the student to locate middle C.)

"The higher ledger lines are easy to remember since the first (lowest) one has the same name as the first letter of the alphabet.

Have the student place an A on that line.

"What note is a third (skip) above A? Right, C. Please place that note in position. Now, a third above C is...? Yes, E."

When all three notes are in place some students may notice that they spell the word ace.

Turn all the notes face down. Point to the notes one at a time and have the student identify each one before he turns it over.

NOTE: In the same or in a later session, add the neighboring space notes as shown. Explain that normally the B below middle C is played with the left hand, but occasionally the right hand "borrows" that note.

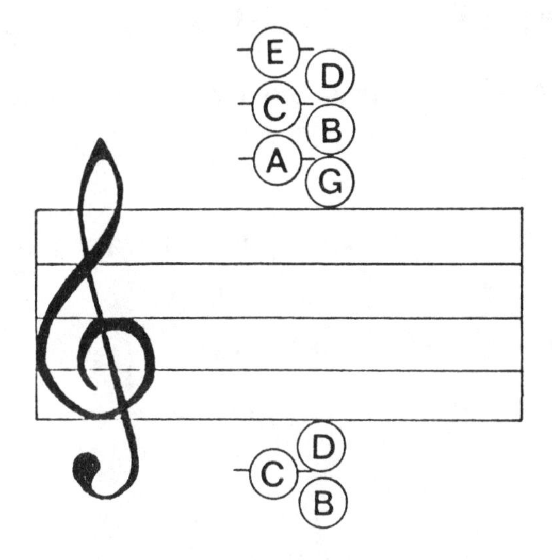

Name This Note I

PURPOSE: To practice naming ledger line notes above and below the treble staff.

TEACHING AIDS: A one-staff board, six popsicle sticks, and notes with names

DIRECTIONS: While the student is out of the room, arrange the sticks and notes as shown below. (The notes are face down.)

Call the student into the room and ask him to identify each note before turning it over to confirm his answer.

Repeat the entire activity several times differing some of the notes each time.

Fun Page - Treble Clef Notes

PURPOSE: To reinforce the fact that each letter is found in two different places on the staff.

TEACHING AIDS: Crayons

DIRECTIONS: The student is to color the notes shown on the next page as directed.

A's - red	D's - yellow	G's - pink
B's - blue	E's - orange	
C's - green	F's - purple	

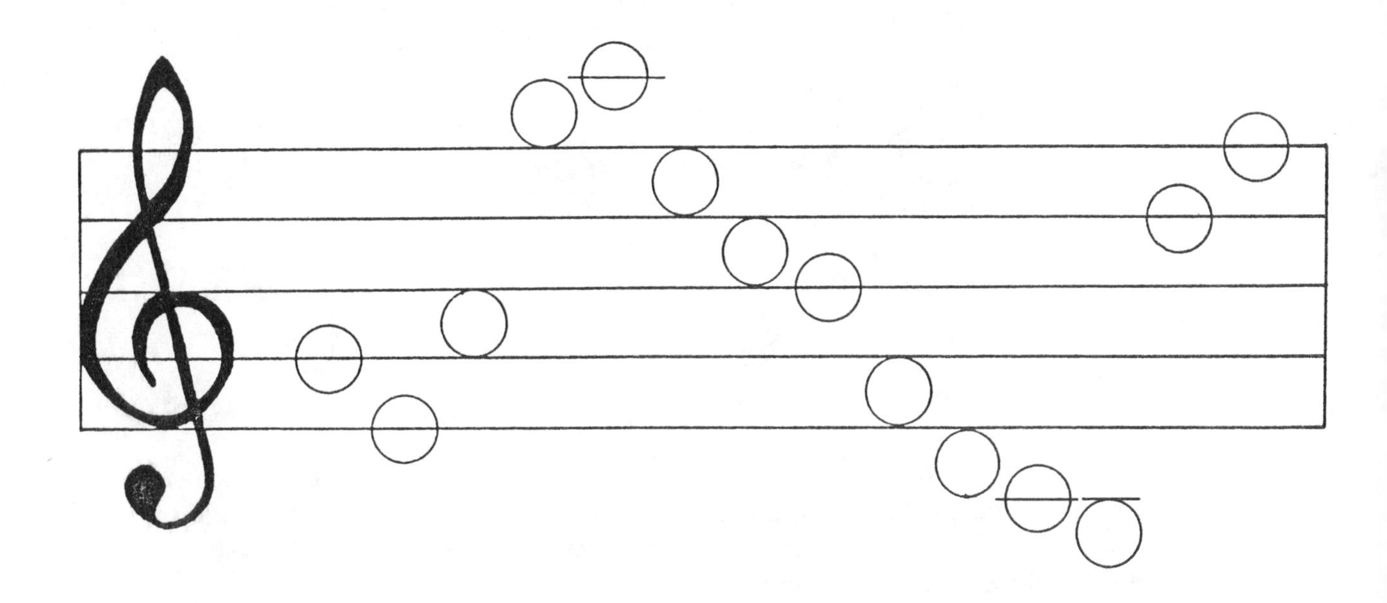

The Bass Clef And Staff

PURPOSE: To review the bass clef and to introduce the line notes of the bass staff.

TEACHING AIDS: A one-staff board and notes with names

DIRECTIONS: Place the staff board on the floor. Explain that the bass clef is also known as the F clef as its position on the staff determines the F line. The clef will always be positioned so that the two dots will be found on either side of the fourth line (counting from the bottom up) in piano music.

To introduce the line notes on the bass staff follow the directions from "JUST LINES." Simply substitute the treble staff and notes with the bass staff and appropriate notes.

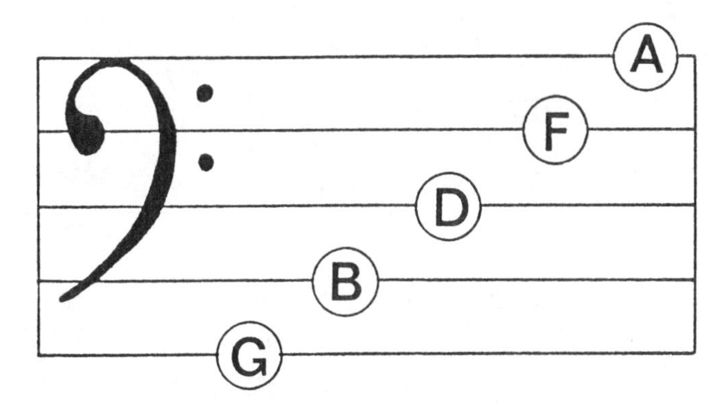

Try a fun association such as "Gee, the lowest line note is no problem to remember." Have fun thinking of other helpful associations of your own.

NOTE: When the student is ready to learn the bass staff space notes, introduce them as you did the treble staff notes in "JUST SPACES."

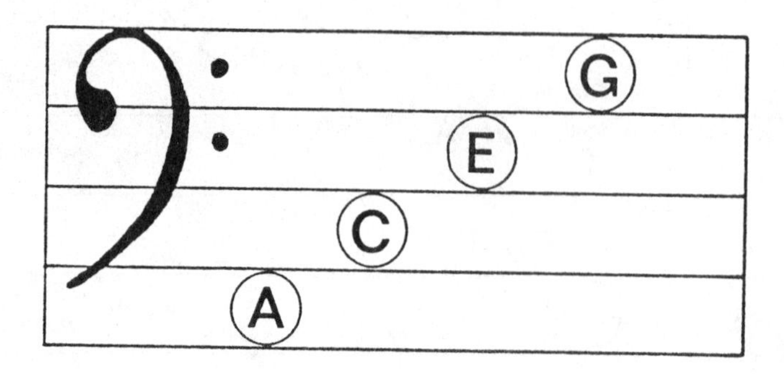

NOTE: To help the student thoroughly memorize the bass clef notes, repeat many of the activities in this Chapter by simply using the bass staff, appropriate notes, and bass clef staff cards as the teaching aids. Slight adjustments may be necessary in one or two activities--feel free to improvise as necessary.

Fun Page - Bass Clef Trucks

PURPOSE: To identify bass clef notes.

TEACHING AID: A pencil

DIRECTIONS: The student is to identify each note. (Very young students may prefer to identify the notes verbally.)

Naming Ledger Line Notes II

PURPOSE: To practice naming the ledger line notes above and below the bass staff.

TEACHING AIDS: A one-staff board, four popsicle sticks, and notes with names

DIRECTIONS: Place the sticks in position as shown on the next page:

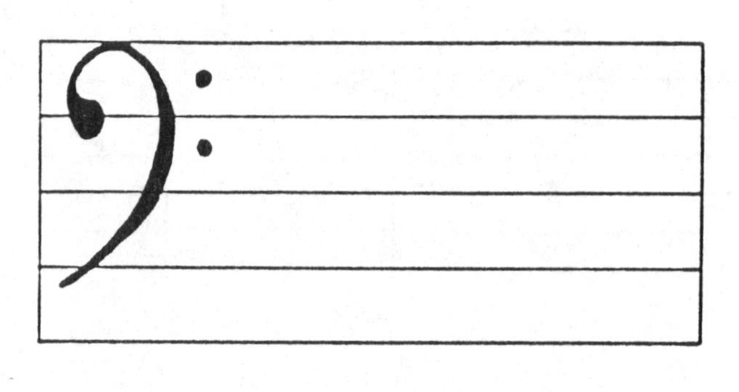

Place a C on the ledger line above the staff. "This note is shared by the treble and bass staffs. You already know its name--middle C."

Place an E on the first ledger line below the staff. Use the by-now-familiar association of the word "e...e...e...easy" with that note.

The student should be able to tell you that C is a third below E and that A is a third below C. Have him place both notes in position as shown below.

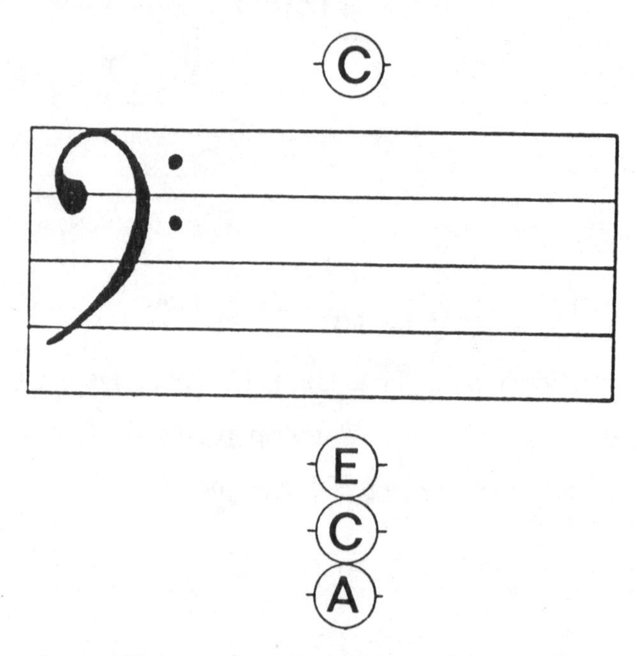

Turn the notes face down. Point to the notes one at a time and have the student identify each one before turning it over to confirm his answer.

NOTE: In the same or at a later session, add the neighboring space notes as shown. Explain that occasionally the left hand "borrows" the D above middle C from the right hand and that is why it is included here.

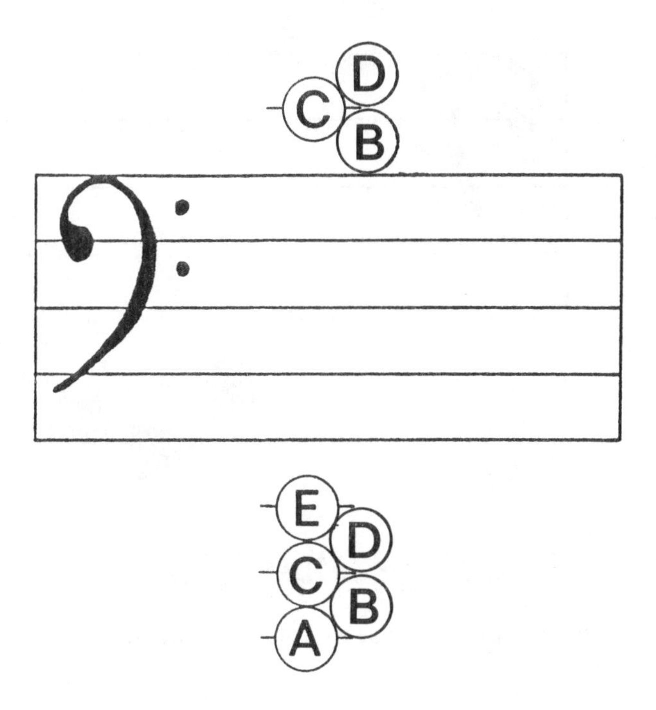

Name This Note II

PURPOSE: To practice naming ledger line notes above and below the bass staff.

TEACHING AIDS: A one-staff board, six popsicle sticks, and notes with names

DIRECTIONS: This activity is just like "NAME THIS NOTE I," except that a bass staff is used (shown on the next page).

Practice naming those notes introduced in "NAMING LEDGER LINE NOTES II."

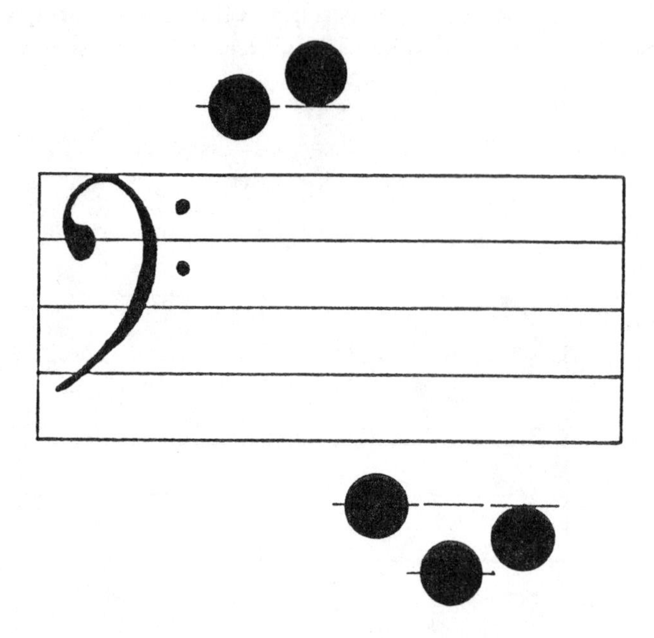

Fun Page - Bass Clef Notes

PURPOSE: To reinforce the fact that each letter is located in two different positions on the staff.

TEACHING AIDS: Crayons

DIRECTIONS: The student is to color the notes shown below as directed.

A's - red	D's - yellow	G's - pink
B's - blue	E's - orange	
C's - green	F's - purple	

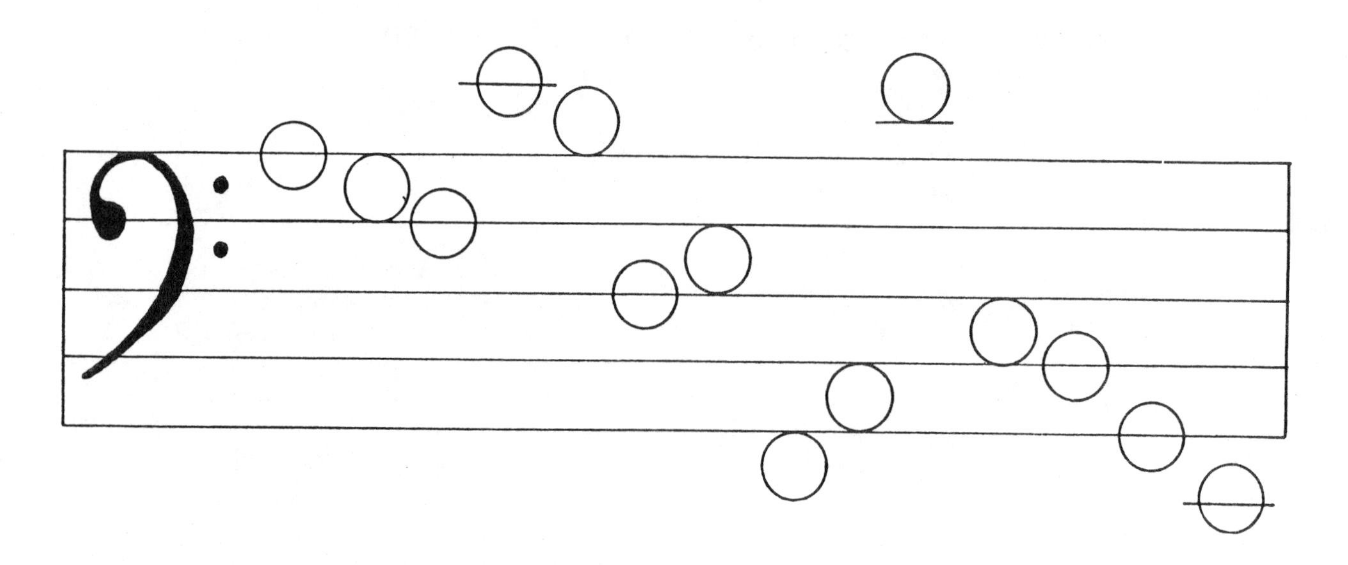

Chapter VII: MUSIC WORDS AND SIGNS

As a student progresses he is exposed to a growing number of music words and signs. As a way of reinforcing the information, some students may enjoy starting a music dictionary of their own to which they can periodically add newly learned material.

In general, words and signs should be introduced as they occur in the music; information introduced before it is pertinent is often quickly forgotten. Make a habit of previewing each new piece with the student by studying the page together to locate any new terms and/or signs and to review the old.

Listed at the end of the Chapter are those words and signs, including definitions, which a student is likely to encounter during his first three years of training. Parents, in particular, may find the list helpful as they help the student with the activities in this Chapter.

Accidentals

PURPOSE: To introduce the student to sharp, flat, and natural signs (which are collectively referred to as accidentals).

TEACHING AIDS: A sharp, flat, and natural card and a piano

NOTE: Students need to be familiar with the term half step and be able to locate half steps at the keyboard.

DIRECTIONS: Stand at the keyboard with the student.

Place the sharp sign on the music rack. Explain that a sharp raises a note one half step.

To demonstrate, play a G and then play G#, the black key just to the right of G.

Encourage the student to find several other G#'s at the keyboard.

Together, practice locating other sharps, including B# (C) and E# (F). Students are often surprised to discover that not all sharps are black keys.

A term which the student may wish to add to his music vocabulary at this time is enharmonic, which refers to a tone which has two spellings. B# and C and E# and F are examples of enharmonic notes.

Next, replace the sharp sign with the flat sign as you explain that a flat lowers a note one half step. The idea that a flat "goes down" like a flat tire is a helpful association.

Help the student to locate and play several flats at the keyboard. Be sure to show him Cb (B) and Fb (E)--more examples of enharmonic notes.

Finally, place the natural sign on the music rack. Explain that this sign is used to cancel a previous sharp or flat.

Rapid Fire

PURPOSE: To have fun reviewing sharps, flats, and naturals at the keyboard.

TEACHING AIDS: A sharp, flat and natural card, two sets of alphabet cards and a piano

DIRECTIONS: Stand at the keyboard with the student.

Place the sharp, flat, and natural cards on the music rack--each approximately a foot apart. Place an alphabet card just to the left of one of the cards. For example, if a G is placed beside the flat card, the student is to locate and play a Gb as quickly as possible. (A letter placed beside the natural sign will correspond to the unaltered key.)

Continue placing the alphabet cards one by one beside either the flat, sharp, or natural card as rapidly as the student can find and play the matching keys.

Dynamic Ducks

PURPOSE: To introduce the student to dynamic symbols.

TEACHING AIDS: Three dynamic ducks - *p, mf,* and *f*

DIRECTIONS: Sit on the floor facing the student.

"I would like to introduce you to the DYNAMIC DUCKS. They tell us how softly or loudly we should play."

Pick up the *p* duck as you say softly, "Here is piano, which means soft in the Italian language. Much beautiful music has come to us over the years from Italy and therefore many of our music terms are Italian as well. Can you say 'piano' with me?" Place the *p* duck on the floor in front of the student.

Next, hand the *mf* duck to the student as you say in a louder voice, "This duck's name is mezzo-forte--say it with me please. Good!" Lay the *mf* duck to the right of the *p* duck.

Finally, hold up the *f* duck as you say loudly "forte." Encourage the student to repeat the term with you. Lay the duck next to the *mf* duck.

Point to the ducks as, together, you and the student say their names at the appropriate voice levels. It is not necessary to define the words <u>mezzo-forte</u> and <u>forte</u>; the student will understand the meanings by the manner in which you say the names. Introduce the other ducks in the same manner as the symbols occur in the music.

NOTE: I chose to introduce these three ducks first as these are the first dynamic symbols the student is likely to encounter.

I have found that the Dynamic Ducks are useful as teaching aids at the practice session or piano lesson. To encourage or remind a student to play a passage softer or louder, I simply place the appropriate duck on the music rack for the duration of the passage. I get immediate results without any words being necessary.

NOTE: The "DYNAMIC DUCKS" is one of three activities included in this book which requires a significant amount of preparation; however, I think you will be rewarded for your investment by the student's enthusiastic response to the ducks.

Crescendo And Decrescendo

PURPOSE: To introduce the terms <u>crescendo</u> and <u>decrescendo</u> and the corresponding signs.

TEACHING AIDS: The crescendo and decrescendo cards and a piano

DIRECTIONS: Stand at the piano with the student and place the crescendo sign on the music rack.

"A crescendo sign tells us to gradually get louder, which is illustrated by the lines growing wider and wider apart."

"I will demonstrate a crescendo for you at the keyboard." Starting with middle C, play the consecutive notes C D E F and G starting softly and growing louder on each note.

Encourage the student to create a crescendo using the same or a different group of five notes.

Next, place the other card on the music rack as you explain that a decrescendo sign means to gradually get softer. "Notice how the lines are far apart and gradually grow closer together." To demonstrate a decrescendo, play middle C loudly and then decrease the loudness of each of the remaining four consecutive notes.

Have the student try a decrescendo of his own.

Finally, explain that you are going to play a group of five white keys which will demonstrate either a crescendo or decrescendo. The student should sit on the floor and place the two cards in front of him. He is to listen carefully to the group of notes, identify it orally as either a crescendo or decrescendo and point to the corresponding card.

Tempo Markings

PURPOSE: To introduce the tempo marking allegretto (or whichever mark occurs first in the music).

TEACHING AIDS: The tempo chart, a pencil, and the student's music book

DIRECTIONS: Sit on the floor with the student.

Open the music book to the student's upcoming piece. Point to the tempo marking, which is found at the top left hand corner directly opposite the composer's name. "Tempo markings indicate how fast or slow a composition or section is to be played. The word tempo means rate of speed. Allegretto indicates that the piece is to be played rather fast."

"The tempo markings are general indicators which allow the performer considerable freedom in his choice of tempo."

"Each time you learn a new tempo marking you may add it to the tempo chart. The order of the markings on the chart is from slowest to fastest. Eventually you will know the order and definitions of all of the most frequently used tempo markings."

Have the student write allegretto and its definition in the seventh position on the Tempo Chart.

NOTE: Shown on the next page is the order of the most common tempo indications. (I referred to the Harvard Brief Dictionary of Music for definitions and order.)

largo (broad)

lento (slow)

adagio (slow)

andante (walking)

andantino (slightly faster than andante)

moderato (moderate)

allegretto (rather fast)

allegro (fast)

vivace (lively)

presto (very fast)

prestissimo (very, very fast)

NOTE: Use the tempo cards in activities such as "FLING'EM" and "HOCUS FOCUS" to review the terms and definitions.

Stairsteps

PURPOSE: To review and introduce music signs.

TEACHING AIDS: Approximately six sign cards and the secret-message card

DIRECTIONS: Deliberately include one or two new signs among the cards.

Place the cards face down on the floor in stairstep fashion with the secret-message card at the top as shown on the next page.

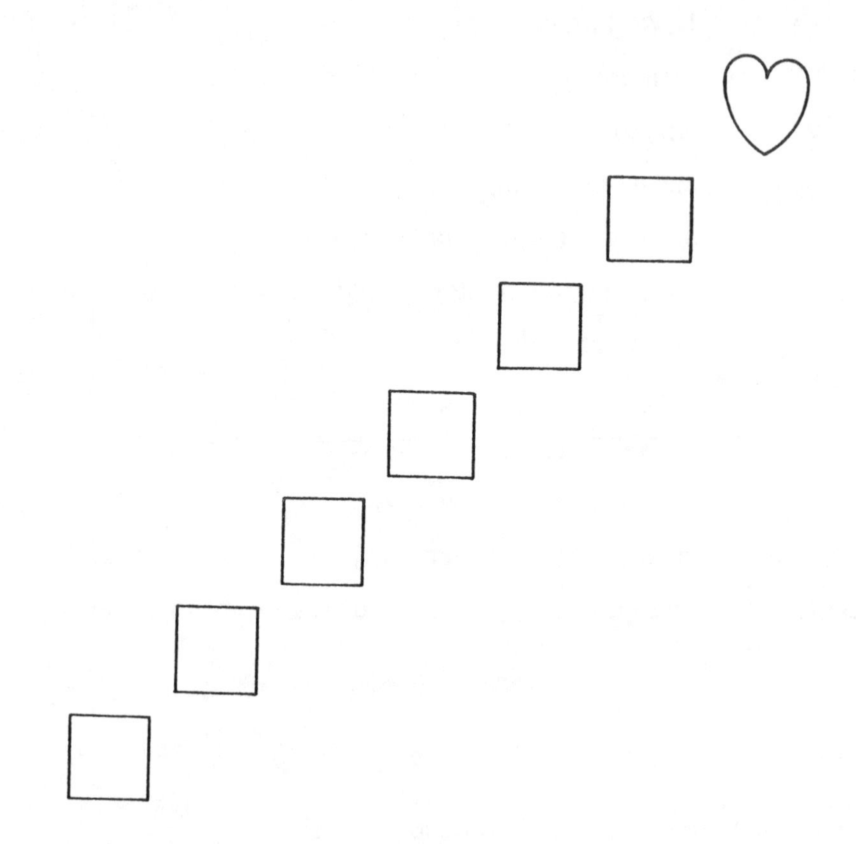

Have the student turn over the first (lowest) card. If he can define the sign, he may proceed up to the next card, continuing in the same manner up to the secret message.

Anytime the student is unfamiliar with a sign take a moment to explain it. Then, have him close his eyes as you rearrange the order of the cards making sure they are all face down once more.

Have the student again start with the first card and work his way to the top. (This time he will know the new sign.)

When he successfully defines all the cards, have him turn over the heart to receive his secret message which might read "Good Work, Billy" or "You deserve a treat for your efforts."

Use a different heart on which is written a new message each time you play.

Children enjoy this game and will want to play it again and again.

Spot A Symbol

PURPOSE: To have fun locating and defining signs and terms in the music.

TEACHING AIDS: One of the student's current piano literature books and a variety of vocabulary and sign cards

DIRECTIONS: Sit on the floor with the student. Scatter the cards near the student. Open the music book to a piece that the student will soon study.

Encourage the student to scan the piece for terms and signs and, as he spots them, to pick up the matching cards. (Plan ahead of time which vocabulary and sign cards will be necessary but include others as well.)

Make certain the student can define each term and sign.

This activity serves as a great preview for new pieces and helps to establish the good habit of studying the page first before playing the piece.

Fling'em

PURPOSE: To have fun reviewing the vocabulary and sign cards.

TEACHING AIDS: A variety of vocabulary and sign cards

DIRECTIONS: Quickly review the cards.

"Now, you are going to do something unusual with these cards. Ordinarily, you are reminded to pick up your toys and keep your room neat, but today I am giving you permission to make a mess!"

Hand the cards to the student and encourage him to fling them up in the air.

Ask the student to pick up and define (one by one) the cards which landed face up. The teacher then collects the cards which landed face down and "acts out" the meanings of those words and signs one at a time for the student, who will have fun guessing the answers and seeing his teacher acting so silly!

Oops!

PURPOSE: To have fun reviewing music signs.

TEACHING AIDS: Approximately seven sign cards and the Oops card, all of the same size and color

DIRECTIONS: Hold the cards as you would a hand of playing cards. Have the student select the cards one by one and identify and define the sign. He wins and keeps the cards which he identifies and defines correctly; however, should a sign be incorrectly identified or defined, take a moment to explain it to the student, then replace the card in your hand so he may have a second opportunity to win it.

The tension and excitement build as the student manages to avoid selecting the Oops card, for once that card is chosen the game must start over again.

Play until the student wins all the cards, leaving the Oops card in your hand.

Hocus Focus

PURPOSE: To have fun reviewing a variety of music terms.

TEACHING AIDS: Approximately ten vocabulary cards and ten matching definition cards of the same size and color

DIRECTIONS: Quickly review the vocabulary cards.

Shuffle them with the definition cards before placing all the cards face down on the floor in four rows with five cards per row.

Have the student point to a card of his choice which you will turn over. Then, ask him to point to another card which he thinks might make a match with the first one. Turn over the second card and, if it does match the first one, the student wins and keeps both cards and earns another turn. If a mismatch occurs, simply return both cards face down and the turn rotates to the other player.

Play until all the matches are made.

Music Vocabulary and Signs

(simple and brief definitions)

Allargando (allarg.) - slowing down and increasing volume

A tempo - return to normal speed

Da capo (D.C.) - to repeat from the beginning to the word fine

Diminuendo (dim. or dimin.) - diminishing

Dolce - sweetly

Espressivo - to play with much expression

Fine - end

Legato - to play without interruption between the notes (connected)

Leggiero - light (soft)

Marcato - marked or emphasized

Poco - little

Rallentando (rall.) - slowing down

Ritardando (rit.) - gradual slowing of speed

Ritenuto - gradual slowing of speed, but often suggesting a marked reduction of speed

Tempo - rate of speed

phrase line

tied notes (the second note is not played, but should be added to the value of the first)

staccato - detached, short

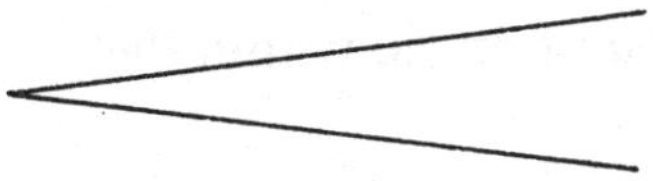

crescendo (cresc.) - gradually grow louder

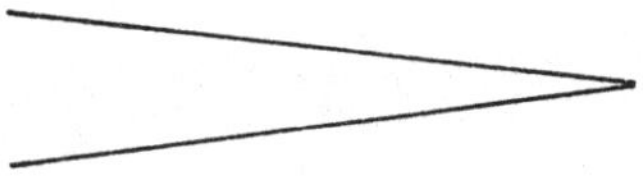

decrescendo (decres.) - gradually grow softer

pp - pianissimo - very soft

p - piano - soft

mp - mezzo-piano - medium soft

mf - mezzo-forte - medium loud

f - forte - loud

ff - fortissimo - very loud

$\frac{2}{4}$	time signature
C ($\frac{4}{4}$)	common time
¢ ($\frac{2}{2}$)	alla breve - a quick duple time with the half note receiving one count
♯	sharp - raises a note one half-step
♭	flat - lowers a note one half-step
♮	natural - cancels the sharp or flat
𝄆 𝄇	repeat signs - repeat the section of music within the signs
𝄐	fermata - hold

accent - to emphasize or stress

grace note - a note printed in small type which is played quickly and does not have a separate time value

key signature

tenuto - sustain the note for its entire time value and occasionally even slightly longer.

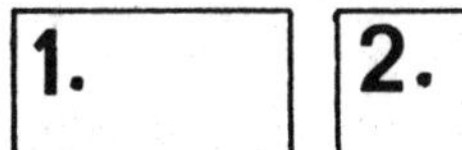

first and second endings

sf - sforzando - strong accent

sharp accent

8va - octava - play one octave higher or lower

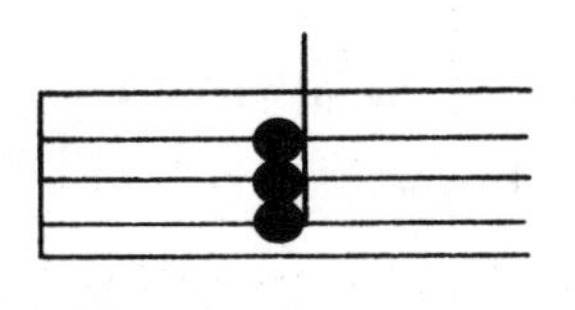

triad - a three-note chord built on thirds (skips)

finger numbers

Chapter VIII: EAR TRAINING

A few musicians are blessed with perfect pitch, but most of us have to practice ear training exercises to develop and improve our ability to hear sounds in a discriminating manner.

The activities found in this Chapter cover the rudimentary ear training skills every beginning pianist should master. Fortunately, it is rarely difficult to get a student to practice the ear training exercises; the activities, aside from being fun, often provide a welcome break from intense practice sessions at the keyboard.

The process of developing one's "ear" requires much repetition, review, and patience. Move slowly, being sure that each exercise is thoroughly mastered before proceeding to the next one.

Finally, impress upon the student how important it is not only to practice the ear training exercises but to listen with great care and concentration while he is playing as well. This ability is an absolute necessity for every good musician to acquire.

High And Low Sounds

PURPOSE: To help the student distinguish between high and low pitches.

TEACHING AID: A piano

DIRECTIONS: Have the student sit with his eyes closed and his back to the piano.

Explain that you will play one note at a time and ask him to identify the sound as either high or low.

Let each note resonate for approximately three or four seconds. At first choose notes that are either very high or very low.

While many students, even very young ones, can easily identify high and low pitches, others consistently reverse their answers. Encourage the latter type of student to "act out" the pitches by standing on tiptoe with his hands raised over his head as you play a high pitch and perhaps fall to a squat position with hands on the floor to represent a low pitch.

Continue to include this activity as part of (or a break from) the home practice session until the student can consistently distinguish between the sounds.

Decaying Sound

PURPOSE: To practice listening to decaying sounds and thereby develop the abilities to concentrate and to listen very carefully.

TEACHING AID: A piano

DIRECTIONS: Sit at the piano with the student.

Explain that you will play a key and keep it depressed to allow the sound to continue resonating. The student is to listen very carefully--focusing his attention only on the sound--and raise his hand at the instant the sound is no longer audible to him.

Explain that on some instruments, such as the violin, the player can maintain the same volume of sound or even increase the loudness by continuing to move the bow over the strings with varying degrees of pressure. The pianist, on the other hand, must realize that once sound is produced it immediately beings to decay.

Some students will be eager to raise their hands too soon. Encourage them to continue following the sound for as long as is possible.

Repeat the exercise several times using keys in different registers.

This is a good listening exercise which requires and develops concentration. Occasionally start the home practice session with this exercise to "set the appropriate mood."

Major And Minor

PURPOSE: To help the student to differentiate between major and minor sounds.

TEACHING AID: A piano

DIRECTIONS: Sit at the keyboard and have the student sit on the floor with his back to the piano.

Explain that you are going to play several triads (three-note chords built on thirds) and you would like him to compare and describe the sounds.

Play three major triads such as C E G, G B D, and D F# A. (First play the notes in each chord singly from the bottom up and then simultaneously before proceeding to the next chord.)

Next, play three minor triads such as C Eb G, G Bb D, and D F A in the same manner.

Have the student describe the difference in the sounds. He may use the word bright to describe the first group of chords and perhaps the word dark to describe the second.

Explain that the term major is used to describe the brighter-sounding group and the word minor to describe the darker-sounding chords.

Tell the student that you are going to play more triads and you would like him to identify each one as either major or minor. (Students can identify the triads more accurately if you play, for example, C major then c minor or g minor then G major, etc. Gradually, and as the student is ready, begin choosing chords in random order from the list shown below.)

Major	Minor
C E G	C Eb G
D F# A	D F A
E G# B	E G B
F A C	F Ab C
G B D	G Bb D
A C# E	A C E
B D# F#	B D F#

Getting Higher Or Lower?

PURPOSE: To help the student to determine if the individual pitches in a group of notes are getting progressively higher or lower.

TEACHING AID: A piano

DIRECTIONS: Have the student sit with his eyes closed with his back to the piano.

Explain that you will play a group of three notes. In a group where the pitches are getting progressively higher, the second pitch will be higher than the first and the third note higher than the second. The reverse will be true for groups in which the pitches are getting lower. Let each note resonate for approximately two seconds being careful not to overlap the sounds of any notes. The student will listen carefully to all three notes before identifying the sounds as either getting higher or lower. (At first, play notes which are at least six or seven notes apart. Gradually, over a period of time and as the student is ready, decrease the distance between the notes until the patterns become groups of consecutive notes.) Remember to play patterns in which the pitches are becoming progressively higher in the low register of the keyboard and vice versa.

Changing Pitches

PURPOSE: To practice identifying changes of pitch.

TEACHING AID: A piano

DIRECTIONS: Have the student seated with his back to the piano and his eyes closed.

Explain that you will play a series of three to five notes. The pattern will be limited to two neighboring pitches and will always begin on the lower pitch. Ask the student if he will raise his hand when he hears the pitch step up and lower it only if he hears the pitch step down.

Hold each note for approximately two seconds. Do not overlap the sounds.

Below are some sample patterns:

C C D   C C C D

C D D C   C D D D

C D C C   C D C D C

Introducing The Intervals Of A Major Scale

PURPOSE: To practice singing and saying the intervals of a major scale.

TEACHING AID: A piano

NOTE: The student should be familiar with and able to spell at least a few major scales.

DIRECTIONS: Sit at the piano with the student.

"Today we are going to sing and say the names of the intervals of a major scale. You remember that an interval is the distance in pitch between two notes."

"Tell me the names of the notes in a C major scale starting with C. That's right, C, D, E, F, G, A, B, C. The first note of a scale is referred to as the perfect prime. In this case which note is the perfect prime? Right, C."

Play middle C up to neighboring D as you sing the letter names on pitch. Be careful not to let the sounds overlap. Play the same notes again as you sing on pitch (one word per note) "major second."

Next, play C up to E singing the letter names and repeating the notes as you sing "major third."

Continue in the same manner with the remaining intervals. Encourage the student to sing the letter and interval names with you.

Intervals of a Major Scale
(using C major as an example)

C - D	=	major second
C - E	=	major third
C - F	=	perfect fourth
C - G	=	perfect fifth
C - A	=	major sixth
C - B	=	major seventh
C - C	=	perfect octave

When you have sung the last interval, go back and sing the entire scale without stopping--"C-D major second, C-E major third, etc." Play the corresponding notes as you sing together.

For reinforcement, have the student spell a D major scale (D E F# G A B C# D). Play and sing the letter and interval names as before.

NOTE: If you wish to practice a scale which is not within a comfortable voice range simply say the letter names and intervals with the student as you play the scale.

Major Seconds And Major Thirds

PURPOSE: To practice identifying major seconds and major thirds aurally.

TEACHING AID: A piano

DIRECTIONS: Sit at the piano and ask the student to sit on the floor facing the piano.

Play middle C up to neighboring D being careful not to allow the sounds to overlap. "We know that this interval is a major second. It is the same interval that we hear between the first two notes of 'Are You Sleeping?'. Let me play the first few notes of that song (C D E C). Can you hear the major second at the beginning?"

Next play C up to E. "C up to E is a major third as you know but did you realize that "Ten Little Indians" begins with that interval? Let me play the first notes of that song (C C C C C C E G G E C)."

"Now, let me play some intervals as you listen with your eyes closed. Identify each interval as either a major second or major third. Compare each interval in your mind to the two songs we discussed. This will help you with your identification."

Play each note soundly letting it resonate for a couple of seconds. Play each interval at least twice. If the student incorrectly identifies an interval play the beginning of the song starting with the correct interval to help him hear the difference.

Below are examples of major seconds and major thirds:

major seconds	major thirds
D up to E	D up to F#
Db up to Eb	E up to G#
E up to F#	F up to A
F up to G	F# up to A#
G up to A	G up to B
A up to B	A up to C#
Bb up to C	B up to D#

Major Seconds, Major Thirds, Perfect Fourths, And Perfect Fifths

PURPOSE: To practice identifying major seconds, major thirds, perfect fourths, and perfect fifths aurally.

TEACHING AID: A piano

DIRECTIONS: Sit at the keyboard and ask the student to sit on the floor facing the piano.

For review, have the student close his eyes as you play a few major second and major thirds for him to identify.

"Now, I am going to add perfect fourths to the intervals which you will identify." Play middle C up to F. "Can you think of some songs which begin with this sound?" The student may suggest "Hark the Herald Angels Sing," "O Christmas Tree," or the wedding song often referred to as "Here Comes the Bride."

Explain that you will play some intervals which will be either major seconds, major thirds, or perfect fourths. The student is to listen carefully with his eyes closed and identify each interval.

Some sample intervals are shown below:

major seconds	major thirds	perfect fourths
C up to D	C up to E	C up to F
D up to E	D up to F#	D up to G
G up to A	G up to B	G up to C
A up to B	A up to C#	A up to D

Finally, add the perfect fifth. Play C up to G. "What is a piece that begins with a perfect fifth?" The most common answer is "Twinkle, Twinkle, Little Star" (C C G G A A G). You and the student may think of other songs as well.

Explain that you will now include perfect fifths among the intervals to be identified. Remember to hold each note approximately two seconds being careful not to overlap the sounds. Play each interval at least twice as the student associates it with the previously mentioned songs.

Some examples of perfect fifths are:

C up to G

E up to B

F# up to C#

A up to E

Repeat this activity using the four intervals over a period of time until the student identifies the majority of the intervals accurately.

Major Sixths, Major Sevenths And Perfect Octaves

PURPOSE: To practice identifying major sixths, major sevenths, and perfect octaves aurally.

TEACHING AID: A piano

DIRECTIONS: Sit at the keyboard and ask the student to sit on the floor facing the piano.

"Today we are going to concentrate on the three remaining intervals of a major scale--major sixths, major sevenths, and perfect octaves. First listen to a major sixth (play middle C up to A). One song which begins with this interval is 'It Came Upon a Midnight Clear'." The first notes of that song are: C A E G F D C D C if you wish to play the opening. The student may know other songs which begin with the same interval.

"The next interval is a major seventh. Listen carefully to the sounds as I play C up to B." Next, play the C and B simultaneously. "This interval as well as the major second (play C and neighboring D simultaneously) are referred to as dissonant intervals." Rather that encourage the student to describe these sounds as "unpleasant" I prefer to describe them as "spicy." I often compare a dissonant interval to the hot sauce one often adds to Mexican foods--it adds flavor and zest.

Finally, have the student listen to the octave (C up to C). A song which begins with this interval and is a great favorite among children as well as adults is "Somewhere Over the Rainbow." If you wish to play the opening notes they are: C C B G A B C. Explain that you are going to play several intervals which the student is to identify as either major sixths, major sevenths, or perfect octaves. Have the student listen with his eyes closed. Immediately correct any inaccurate identifications.

Some examples of the three intervals are listed below:

major sixths	major sevenths	perfect octaves
C up to A	C up to B	C up to C
D up to B	F up to E	D up to D
F up to D	G up to F#	E up to E
G up to E	A up to G#	F up to F

Interval Scramble

PURPOSE: To practice identifying all the intervals of a major scale aurally.

TEACHING AID: A piano

DIRECTIONS: Ask the student to sit on the floor with his back to the piano and with his eyes closed.

Explain that you will play intervals from various major scales--from major seconds up to and including perfect octaves. The student is to identify each interval as a major second, major third, perfect fourth, etc.

You may wish to quickly review each interval and recall any association with a song you may have made previously.

Immediately, but gently, correct any inaccurate identifications before proceeding to the next interval.

Repeat the entire activity on several occasions as part of (or a break from) the home practice session.

Listed below are examples of intervals from various major scales:

major seconds	major thirds	perfect fourths
D up to E	C up to E	C up to F
G up to A	F up to A	D up to G
A up to B	G up to B	F up to Bb
B up to C#	A up to C#	G up to C

perfect fifths	major sixths	major sevenths
C up to G	C up to A	C up to B
F up to C	D up to B	D up to C#
G up to D	F up to D	F up to E
A up to E	G up to E	G up to F#

perfect octaves
C up to C
E up to E
F# up to F#
G up to G

Chapter IX: MAJOR SCALES

In this Chapter the student will be introduced to pentachords and major scales. He will become familiar with the pattern of whole and half steps on which major scales are built, as well as the circle of fifths, which illustrates the relationship between the scales.

C major scale and scales having sharps in the key signature are introduced first. The student should master these before proceeding to the scales containing flats.

The activities are designed to make understanding scales, practicing them at the keyboard, and memorizing the key signatures fun and easy. As the student masters the information, he is paving the way for learning the minor scales later.

Pentachords

PURPOSE: To introduce the first five notes of the major scales.

TEACHING AIDS: One set of alphabet cards, several whole- and half-step cards and a piano

NOTE: The student should be able to identify half and whole steps at the keyboard.

DIRECTIONS: Sit on the floor with the student.

"Today I am going to show you an easy way to determine the first five notes of any major scale. You will hear me refer to these groups of five notes as pentachords. Can you say that? Good. Penta means five, so pentachords must be built of five notes."

"There is a formula for building major pentachords which I am going to let you discover."

Lay the cards on the floor as shown below:

"Is the distance between C and D a half or whole step? (The student may refer to the keyboard if he wishes.) Right, a whole step." Place a whole step card in position.

"Now, what is the distance between D and E? Yes, another whole step." Have the student place the whole step card in position as shown below:

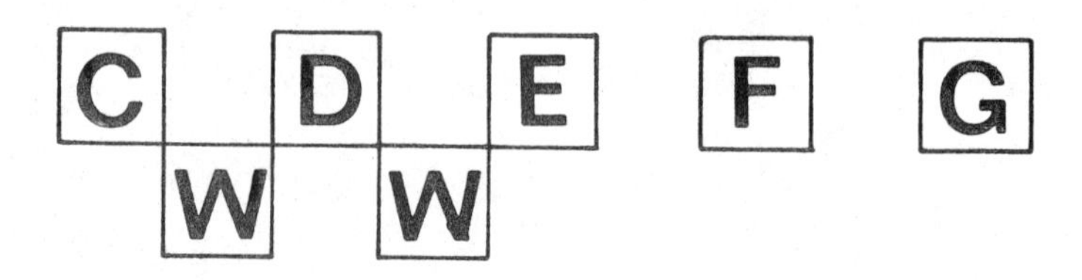

Continue in the same manner with E and F which is a half step and F and G which is a whole step.

The finished pentachord should look like this:

"You have discovered the formula for building the first five notes of any major scale--whole step, whole step, half step, whole step."

Take the student to the piano and let him play a C major pentachord with the right hand. Place his thumb on a C. Encourage him to use fingers 1-5 as he plays each note singly ascending and descending.

Next, place the student's thumb on a G. "I'll bet you can play a pentachord starting with G. Let's use our formula to determine the remaining notes. What note is a whole step above G? Right, A. A whole step above A is.....yes, B. Which note is a half step above B? Right again, C. The last note, a whole step above C, is.....great, D. So, we have discovered that the notes in a G major pentachord are G, A, B, C, and D."

Encourage the student to play the pentachord as before.

NOTE: In another session introduce the remaining pentachords which begin on white keys--D, E, F, A, and B. (All of the major pentachord patterns are listed below and on the following page.) I would suggest demonstrating these at the keyboard for the student and then letting him try them. It is not necessary to take the time to use the formula to determine each pattern but I believe it is important for the student to understand that a pattern exists and that it remains constant in each pentachord.

Finally, in a later session introduce the pentachords starting on black keys (Db, Eb, Gb, Ab, and Bb). The student will enjoy the challenge of playing these patterns.

When the student has mastered each pattern encourage him to practice them chromatically--which means to move by half steps. He will begin with C major, proceed to the pattern starting on Db, then to D, etc.

Major Pentachord Patterns

C D E F G

Db Eb F Gb Ab

D E F# G A

Eb F G Ab Bb

E F# G# A B

F G A Bb C

Gb Ab Bb Cb Db

G A B C D

Ab Bb C Db Eb

A B C# D E

Bb C D Eb F

B C# D# E F#

Major Scales

PURPOSE: To introduce major scales.

TEACHING AIDS: Two sets of alphabet cards, several whole- and half-step cards and a sharp card

DIRECTIONS: Sit on the floor with the student.

Explain that you are going to build a major scale which is a succession of seven different notes determined by a particular pattern of whole and half steps.

Lay the first five notes of a C major scale on the floor leaving some space between each of the cards.

"You are already familiar with the major pentachords which are the first five notes of the major scales. Can you quickly tell me the pattern of whole and half steps? Right, whole, whole, half, and whole."

Arrange the cards as shown below:

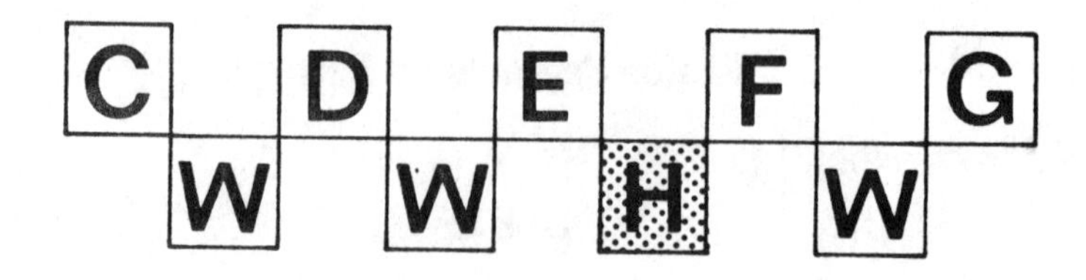

"Now, all we have to do is to determine the remaining three letters. Let me help you by completing the pattern of whole and half steps."

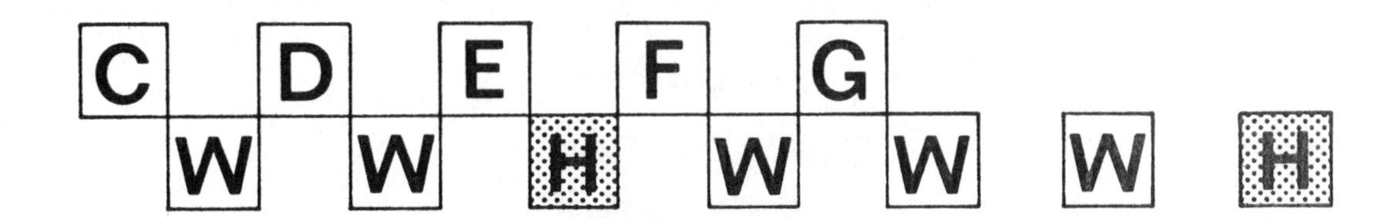

"Can you tell me the note a whole step above G? Yes, A." Have the student place the A in position.

"A whole step above A is.....yes, B and what note is a half step above B? Right C." Place the remaining cards in order.

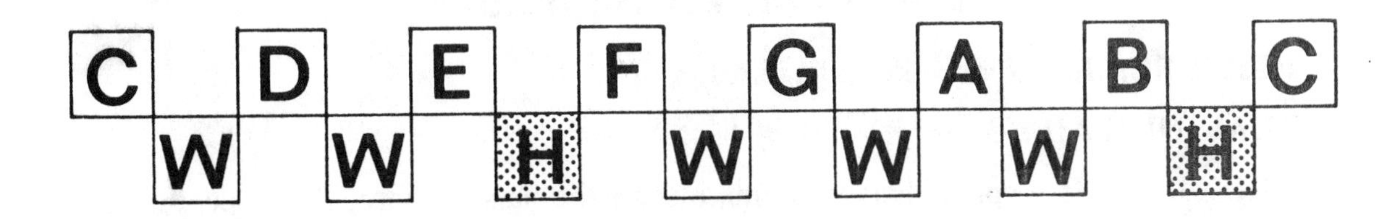

Starting with C, say aloud together the letters of the C major scale.

"How many whole steps are in a major scale? Right, five. How many half steps do you see? Yes, two."

Quickly remove only the alphabet cards and place a G above and to the left of the first whole step card.

Help the student to build a G major scale using the half and whole step cards as a guide. Remember that the seventh note will be F#; add the sharp sign above F as shown:

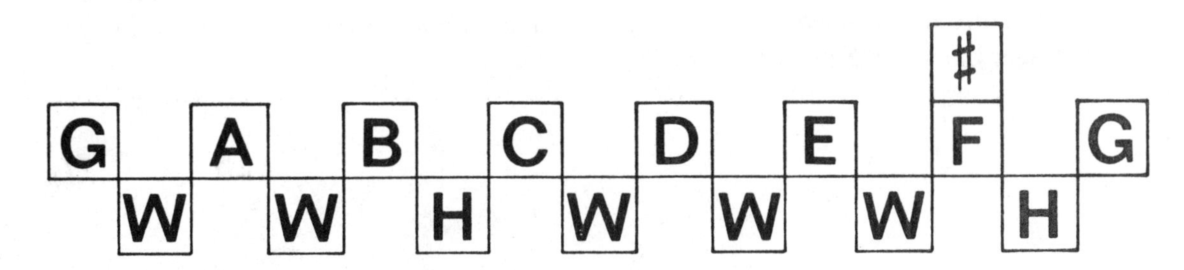

Say the scale aloud together.

"Now, you know the formula (whole, whole, half, whole, whole, whole, half) which will allow you to build any major scale.

NOTE: In another session you may wish to build other scales or help the student to play them at the piano.

Listed on the next page are the remaining major scales which have sharps in the key signature.

D E F# G A B C# D

A B C# D E F# G# A

E F# G# A B C# D# E

B C# D# E F# G# A# B

F# G# A# B C# D# E# F#

C# D# E# F# G# A# B# C#

Focus On Key Signatures

PURPOSE: To introduce key signatures.

TEACHING AID: A pencil

DIRECTIONS: Explain that key signatures are the flats or sharps that appear on the staff at the beginning of a piece which indicate the scale and key.

The major scales having sharps in the key signature are listed below in order starting with the scale having only one sharp to the scale having seven.

The sharps occur in the scales in a particular order; F, C, G, D, A, E, and B. In the beginning, the student will enjoy learning this fun jingle to aid in the memorization of the sharps: fried chicken, good dumplings, and even biscuits. Also, daily scale practice at the keyboard will help to reinforce the key signatures.

On the next page have the student add sharps over the appropriate letters in each scale; the scale of G has one sharp (F), the scale of D has two (F and C), etc. He may notice as he does this that a pattern emerges. The new sharp in each successive scale is always added over the seventh degree.

G	A	B	C	D	E	F♯	G
D	E	F	G	A	B	C	D
A	B	C	D	E	F	G	A
E	F	G	A	B	C	D	E
B	C	D	E	F	G	A	B
F	G	A	B	C	D	E	F
C	D	E	F	G	A	B	C

Roll And Name Key Signatures

PURPOSE: To review major scales containing sharps in the key signature.

TEACHING AIDS: One set of alphabet cards, two sharp cards and a die

DIRECTIONS: Place the alphabet cards on the floor as shown below:

G	D	A	E	B	♯ F	♯ C

The order is determined by the number of sharps in the key signature (G has one, D has two, etc.).

Have the student roll the die. If, for example, he rolls a four he must identify the scale having a key signature of four sharps (E major) and name the sharps in order (F, C, G, D).

Encourage the student to use the jingle to help him name the sharps.

Next, the teacher rolls the die, identifies the corresponding scale and names the sharps in order.

If either of you gives an incorrect answer, gently correct one another and continue with the activity.

Also, if either of you rolls the same number as was rolled by the other player on the previous roll, you automatically name the scale having seven sharps as its key signature and then name the sharps in order.

To make the game more challenging, scramble the order of the cards on the floor.

NOTE: At the appropriate time use this activity to review major scales containing flats.

Place the cards in order, according to the number of flats, as shown below:

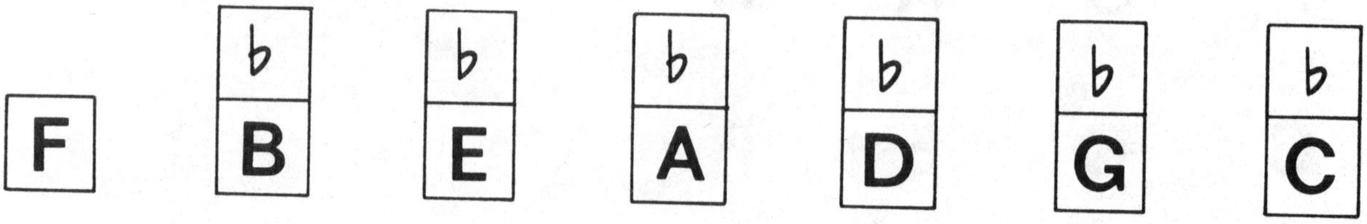

F	♭ B	♭ E	♭ A	♭ D	♭ G	♭ C

Key Signature Slap Down

PURPOSE: To have fun identifying key signatures.

TEACHING AIDS: Key signature cards and two sets of alphabet cards

DIRECTIONS: This game is played just like "SLAP DOWN" found in Chapter VI. Simply replace the staff cards with key signature cards and follow the same directions.

Sometimes, review just the scales having sharps in the key signature, and other times practice just the scales containing flats.

Fun Page - Sharps On The Staff

PURPOSE: To introduce the placement of sharps on the staff and to practice writing them.

TEACHING AID: A pencil

DIRECTIONS: Study together the illustration shown below:

"You know the order of the sharps is F, C, G, D, A, E, and B. Notice that the sharp on the far left is on the F line, the next sharp on the C space, and so on."

"When you write the sharps on the staff you must be careful to maintain the order."

Using the illustration shown above as a guide, have the student write the sharps on the staff. The center of each sharp should be exactly on a line or space.

Fun Page - Major Scales I

PURPOSE: To practice writing scales containing sharps on the staff.

TEACHING AID: A pencil

DIRECTIONS: Below and on the following page, the student is to write the designated scale on the staff including any necessary sharps. (The sharp sign is placed to the left of the note which it is altering.)

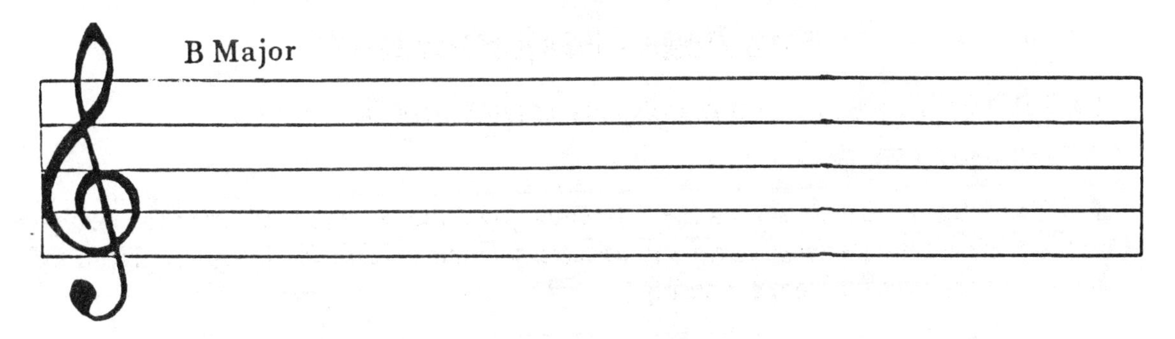

Fun Page - Key Signatures I

PURPOSE: To identify the key signatures of various major scales.

TEACHING AID: A pencil

DIRECTIONS: The student is to identify the scale which corresponds to each key signature.

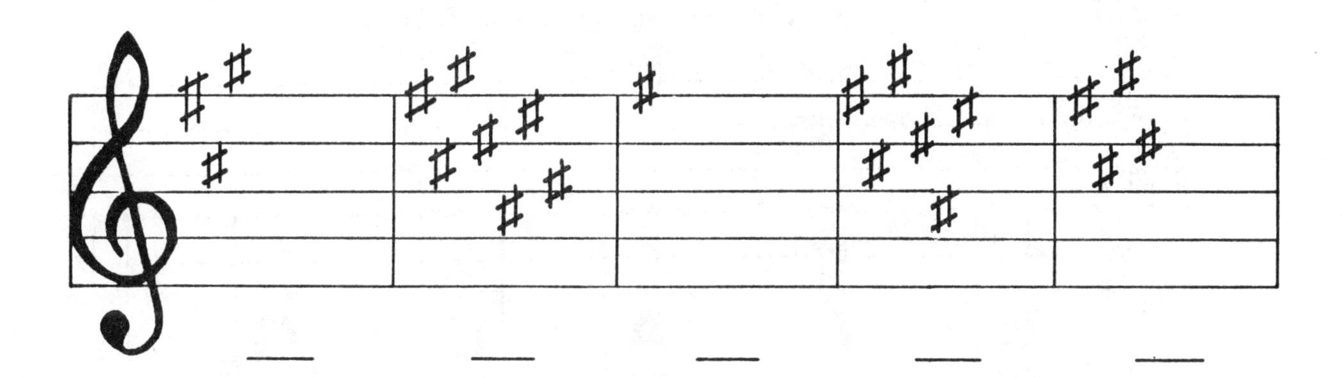

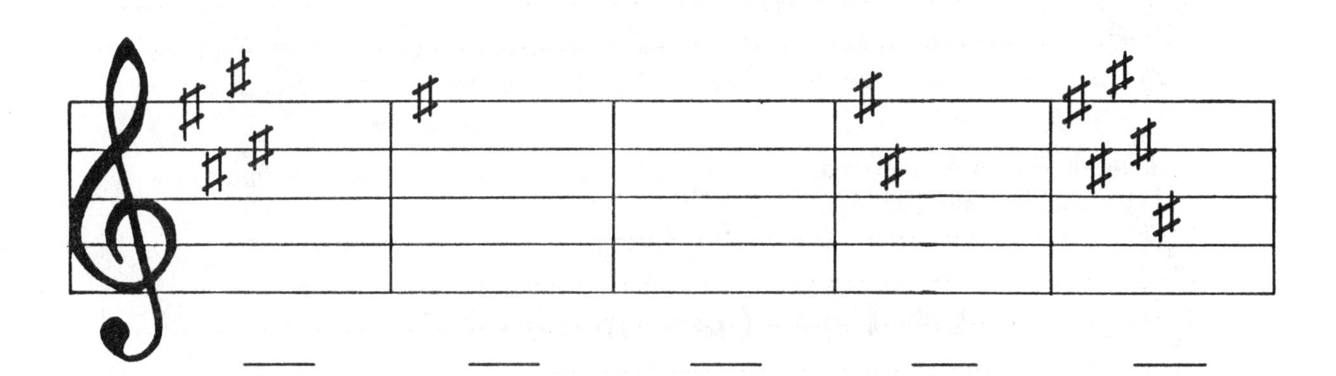

Have the student write the appropriate key signatures on the staff.

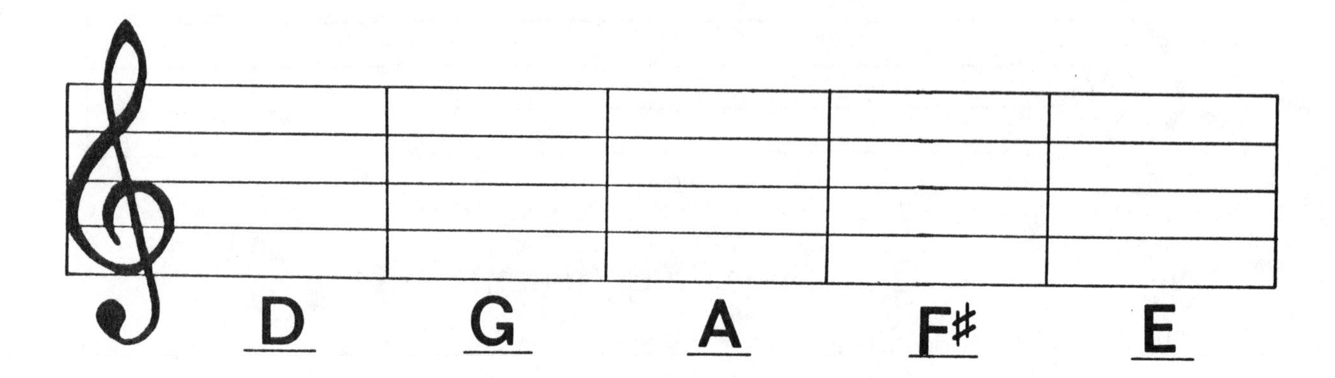

Scales With Flats In The Key Signature

PURPOSE: To introduce major scales containing flats.

TEACHING AIDS: One set of alphabet cards and several flat cards

DIRECTIONS: Sit on the floor with the student.

Arrange the cards as shown below:

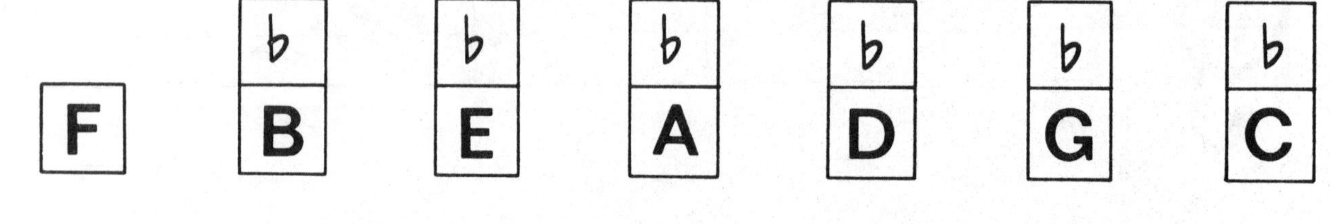

"The order of the flats is B, E, A, D, G, C, and F. An easy way to remember the flats is to notice that the first four spell the word bead. To remember the last three I simply think of gold colored fish.

"The cards are in order according to the number of flats in the key signature. F major has one flat--B, Bb major has two flats--B and E. Bb, Eb, and Ab are found in an Eb major scale and so on.

"I am going to point to a letter and I need you to tell me how many flats are in the key signature and then name them in order."

Fun Page - Flats On The Staff

PURPOSE: To introduce the placement of flats on the staff and to practice writing them.

TEACHING AID: A pencil

DIRECTIONS: Study together the illustration shown below:

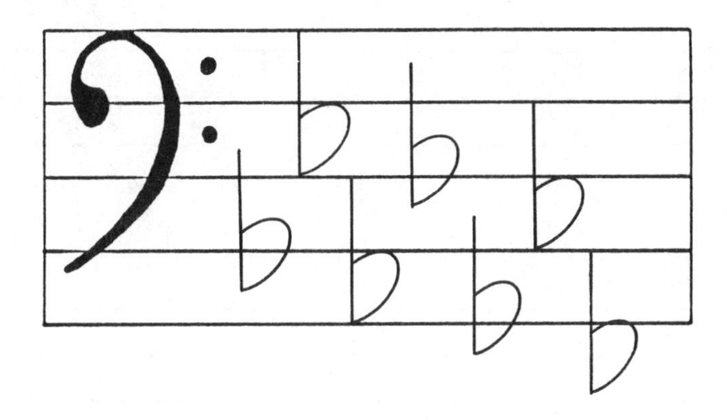

"You know the order of the flats is B, E, A, D, G, C and F. Notice that the flat on the far left is on the B line, the next flat is on the E space, and so on."

"When you write the flats on the staff you must be careful to maintain the order."

Using the illustration shown above as a guide, have the student write the flats on the staff. The center of each flat should be exactly on a line or space.

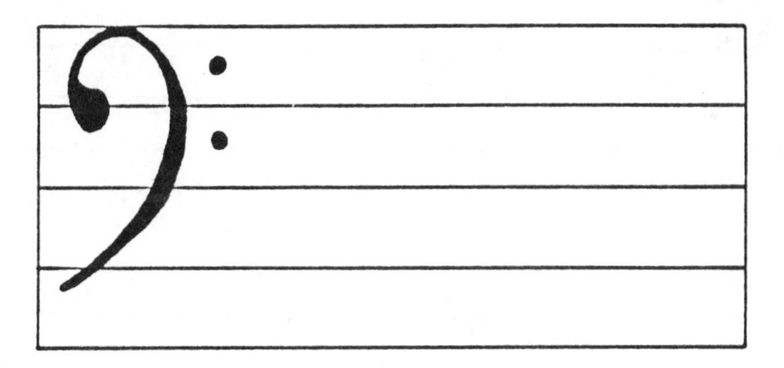

Fun Page - Major Scales II

PURPOSE: To practice writing scales containing flats on the staff.

TEACHING AID: A pencil

DIRECTIONS: Using the illustration on the next page, the student is to write the designated scale on the staff including any necessary flats (the flat sign is placed to the left of the note which it is altering).

F Major
B♭ Major
E♭ Major
A♭ Major
D♭ Major

Fun Page - Key Signatures II

PURPOSE: To identify the key signatures of various major scales containing flats.

TEACHING AID: A pencil

DIRECTIONS: The student is to identify the scale which corresponds to each key signature.

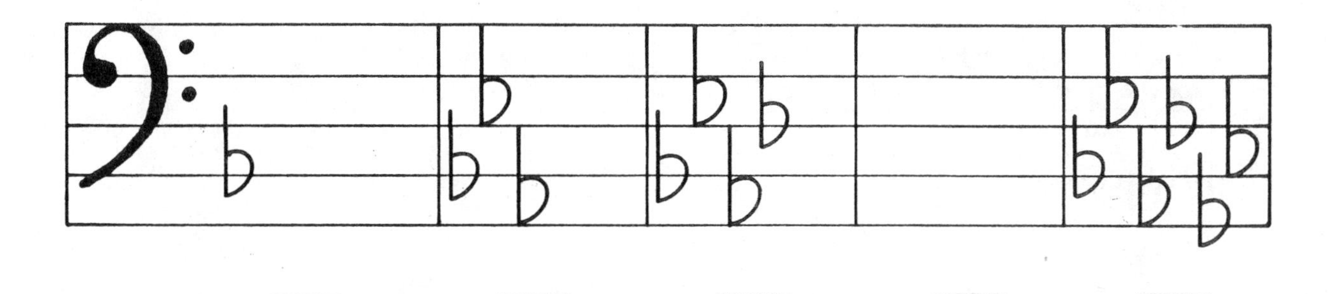

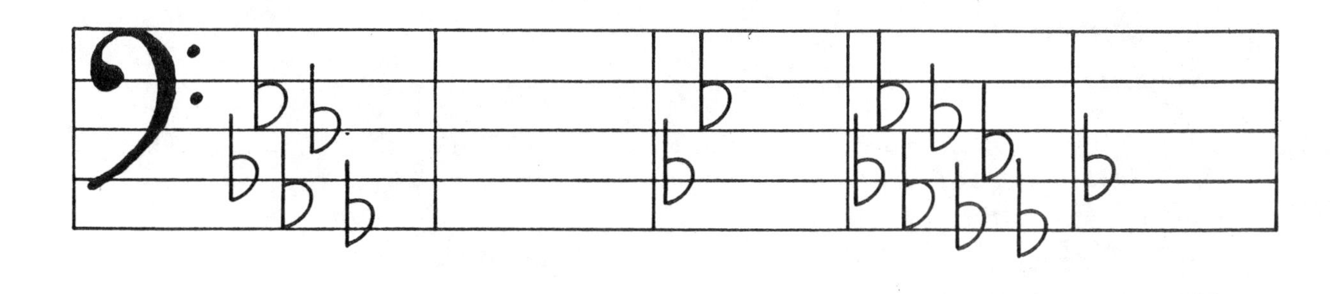

Have the student write the appropriate key signatures on the staff.

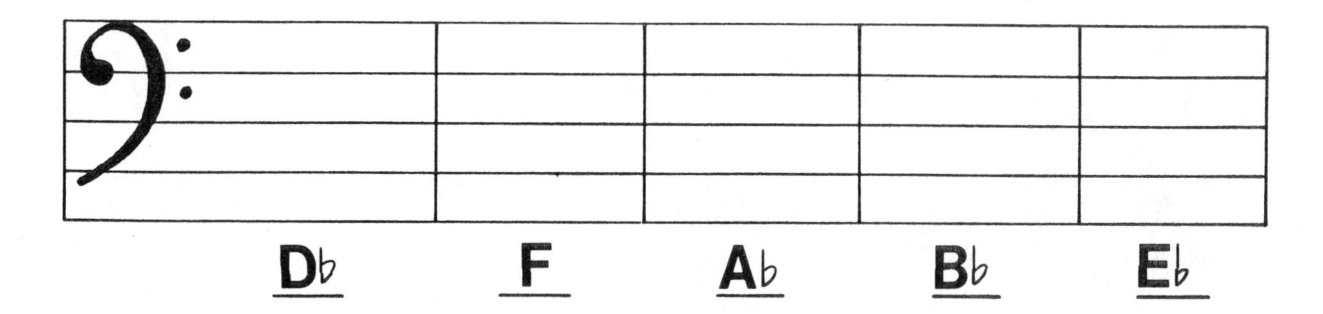

Key Signatures In The Music

PURPOSE: To practice locating and identifying key signatures in various pieces.

TEACHING AID: One of the student's music books

NOTE: Before helping the student with this exercise, ask the student's piano teacher to scan the book and mark any pieces in minor keys which you will want to skip over for the purpose of this activity.

DIRECTIONS: Explain that before playing a new piece one should always first check the key signature and time signature. The key signature will be found just to the left of the time signature. If there are no sharps or flat there assume, for now, the piece is in the key of C major.

Help the student to determine the key of various pieces in the book.

Circle Of Fifths

PURPOSE: To introduce the circle of fifths.

TEACHING AIDS: None

DIRECTIONS: Together, study the circle of fifths shown on the next page.

"Many music theorists use the circle of fifths to illustrate in a simple way the relationship which exists between the major scales. C major has no sharps and no flats in its key signature. Now, start with C and count up five letters. What letter do you come to? Right, G. (Point to each letter as it is discussed.) G is the major scale that has one sharp as its key signature. Now, count up five letters starting with G. Yes, you come to D, which has two sharps in the key signature. Let's keep going--five letters above D is .....? Right, A. Guess how many sharps A has. Right again, three."

"Do you see the pattern that is beginning to emerge? We can continue in this manner until we arrive at C# major which has seven sharps. If we go back to C at the top and count down (or backward) five letters we come up to F which has one flat, B. A fifth below F is Bb which has two flats in its key signature and so on to Cb which has seven flats."

"Notice that three keys overlap on the circle of fifths--B and Cb, F# and Gb, and C# and Db. These scales are described as enharmonic; this means that they sound the same but are spelled differently."

For reinforcement, point to different letters on the circle of fifths and have the student tell you the number of sharps or flats in the key signature and then name them in order.

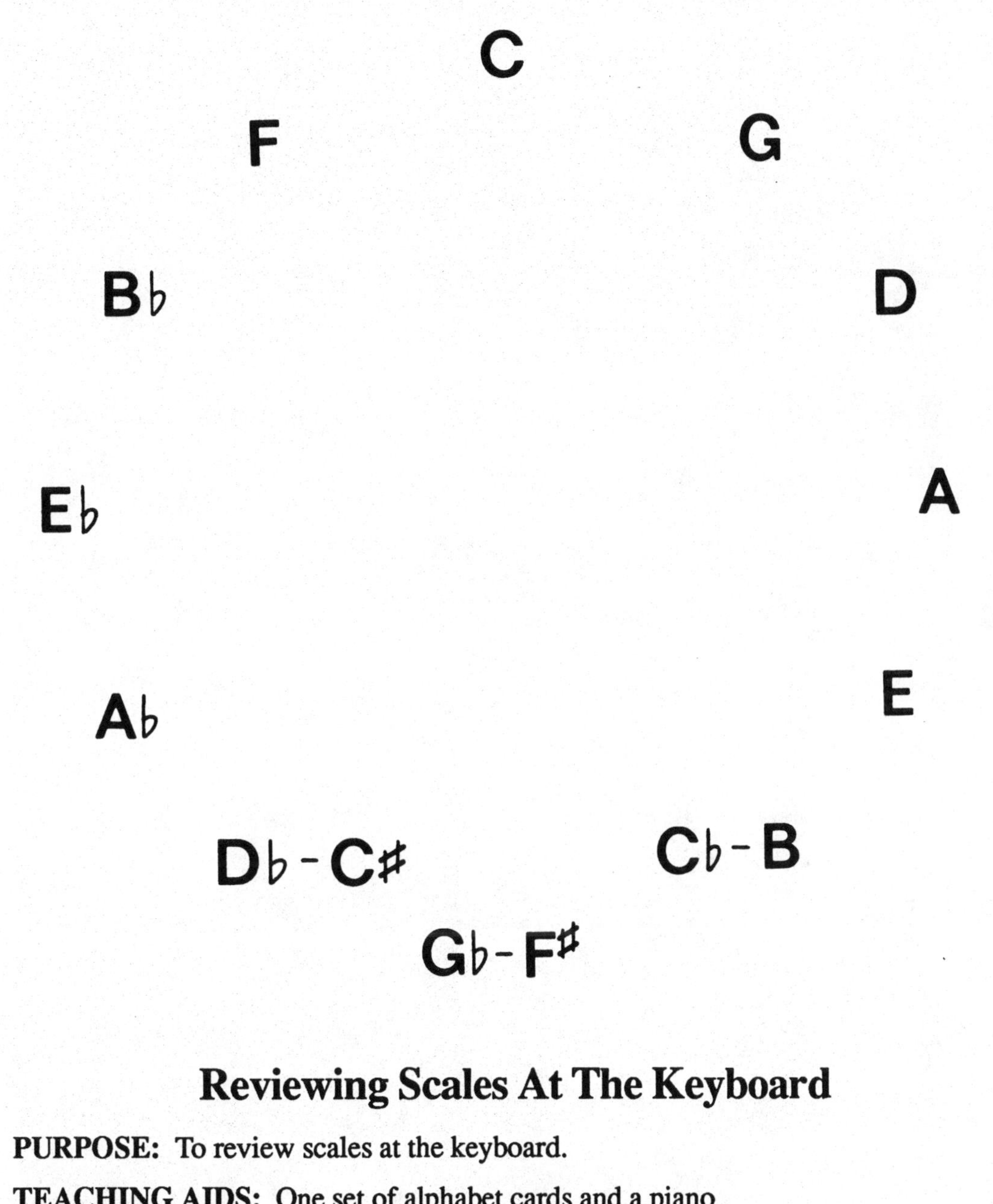

Reviewing Scales At The Keyboard

PURPOSE: To review scales at the keyboard.

TEACHING AIDS: One set of alphabet cards and a piano

DIRECTIONS: The student should be seated at the piano.

Choose those alphabet cards which represent the keys you wish to review and lay the others aside.

Hold the cards as you would a hand of playing cards. Have the student choose one card, identify the key signature of that scale, and then play it.

Continue in the same manner with the remaining cards.

E

A

D [illegible] Cb [illegible]

Gb [illegible]

Recreating Scales: A Line [illegible]

[illegible]

DIRECTIONS: [illegible]

DIRECTIONS: [illegible] should be [illegible] of the page.

[illegible]

[illegible] hand [illegible] The [illegible]

[illegible] marking [illegible]

Description of Teaching Aids

Construction paper in a variety of colors, a felt-tip pen, and scissors are all you need to make most of the teaching aids.

1. Alphabet cards - each set of cards may be of a different color. Make the cards approximately four inches square. The maximum needed is four sets.

2. Music Train - See the patterns on pages 113 and 115. You will need seven cars and one engine. If you use white construction paper, have fun coloring the detail work of each car in a variety of colors (or simply cut each car from a different color of paper). Write one of the music alphabet letters in the center of each car. Color and write "Music Train" on both sides of the engine.

3. One-staff board - Use poster board. If you wish, refer to pages 17 and 19 before drawing the clef signs. The lines of the staff should be approximately two inches apart.

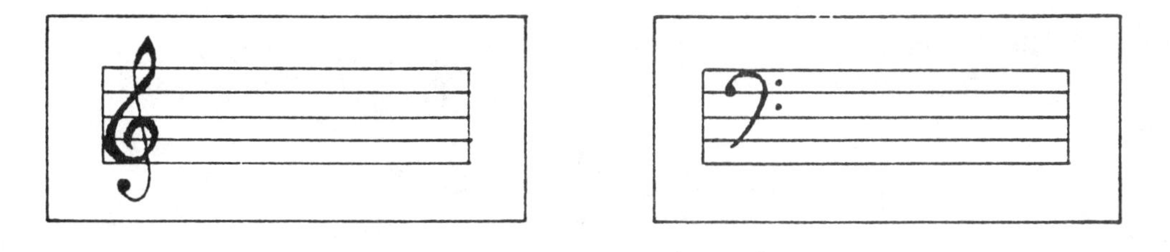

4. Plain notes (all of the same color and sized to fit between lines on the staff boards). The maximum needed is ten.

5. Staff cards - Either make these yourself or purchase them at a music store; however, for some activities the staff cards cannot have the answer (alphabet letter) on the back. Check cards for this feature before buying.

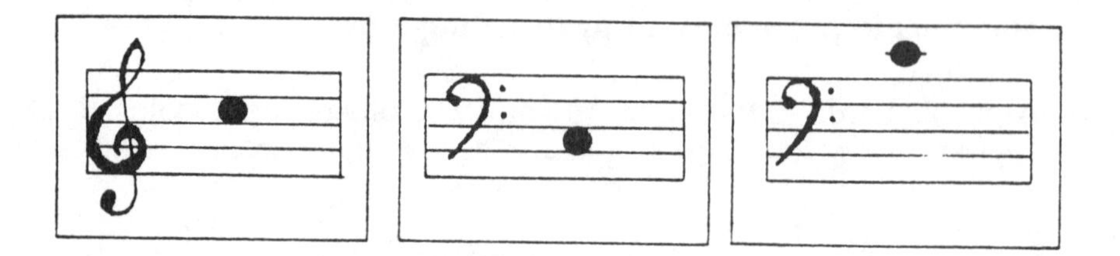

6. Two-staff board - Use poster board. The lines should be approximately two inches apart.

7. Rhythm cards - Using white construction paper, draw the notes and rest in the designated colors. Make six of each of the time values shown below.

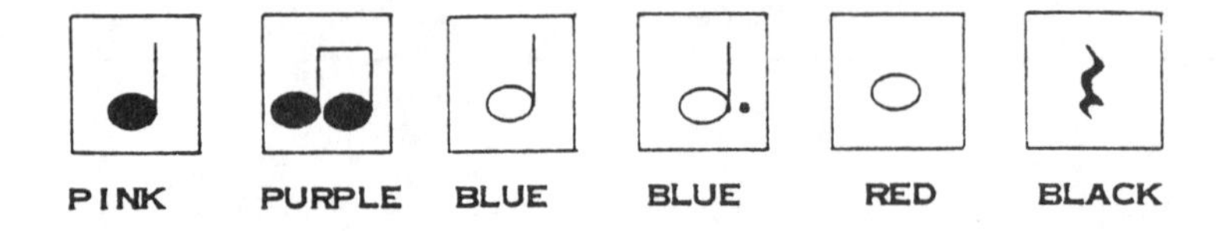

8. Time signature cards -

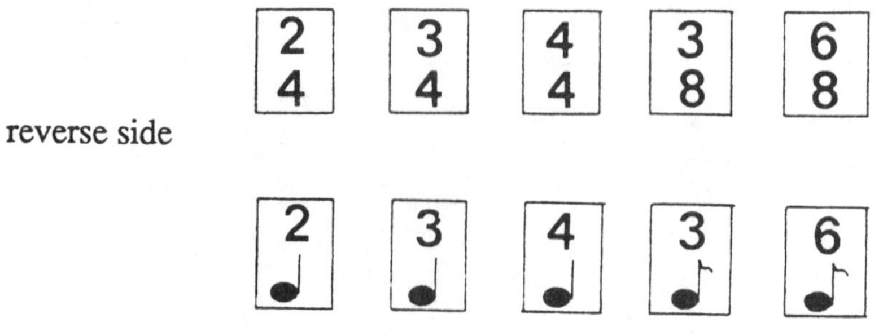

9. Got'cha card - The same size and color as the alphabet cards.

Got'cha

10. Notes with names - All of the same color, sized to fit between lines on the staff. Make two of each alphabet letter.

E

A C

11. Sad Cecil - Same size and color as the notes with names. Make approximately three or four.

12. Sharp card (black on green, same size as alphabet cards) - Make seven cards.

13. Flat card (black on yellow, same size as alphabet cards) - Make seven cards.

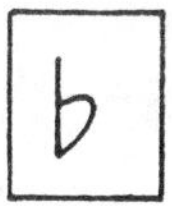

14. Natural card (black on red, same size as alphabet cards) - Make one card.

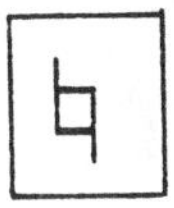

15. Dynamic Ducks - See patterns on pages 117 through 127. Cut the ducks from yellow construction paper. Detail as you wish.

16. Crescendo card -

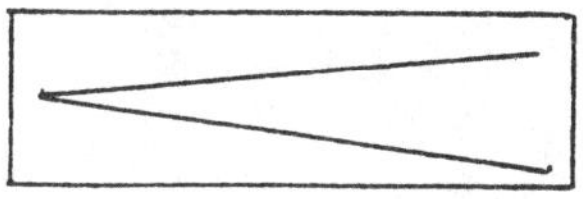

17. Decrescendo card -

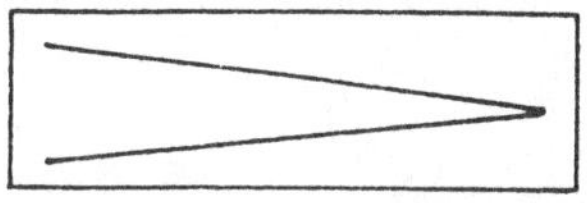

18. Tempo chart - Use a sheet of construction paper in the student's favorite color.

TEMPO CHART

1
2
3
4
5
6
7
8
9
10
11

19. Sign cards (all of the same color).

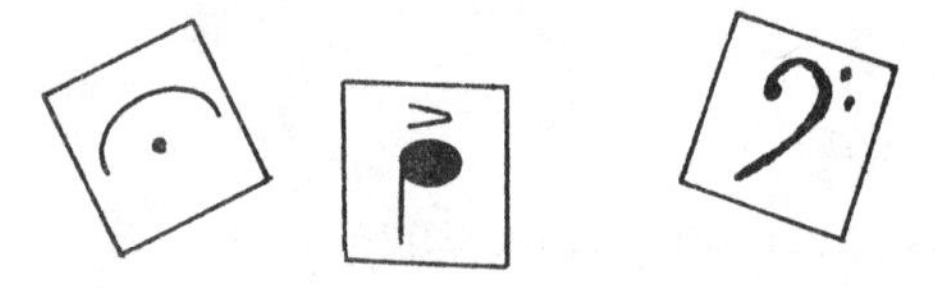

20. Secret-message card (red) - 

21. Note die - I made the die from a cracker box, cutting it so it would be equally square on every side. I covered it in brown wrapping paper and wrote one of the figures shown below on each side.

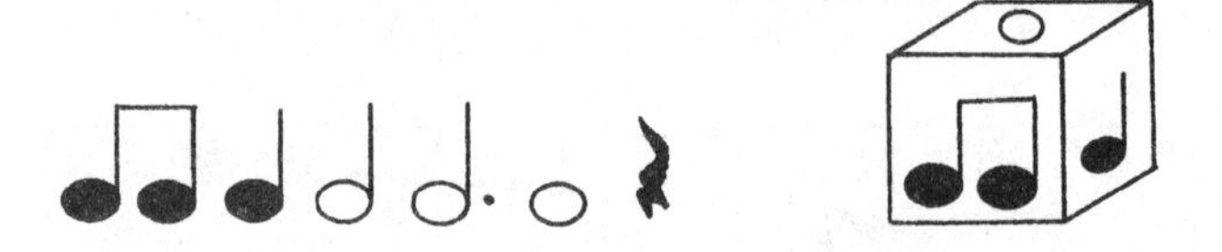

22. Vocabulary and definition cards (orange, all the same size). Refer to pp. 74-76

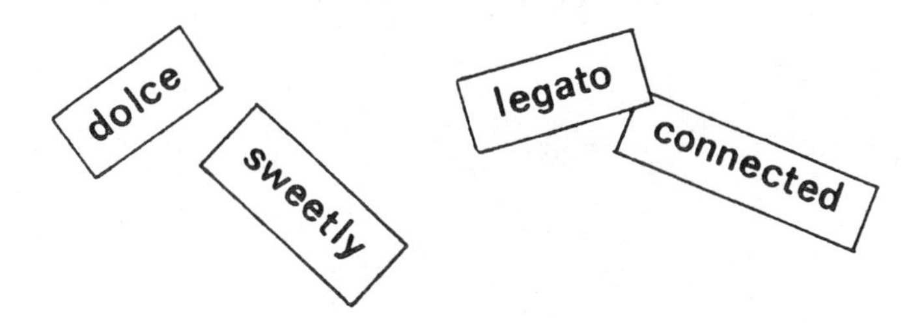

23. Tempo cards - Refer to p. 71

largo   presto

24. Sign cards - (yellow, all the same size). Refer to pp. 75-77.

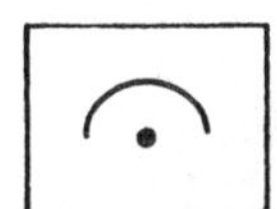

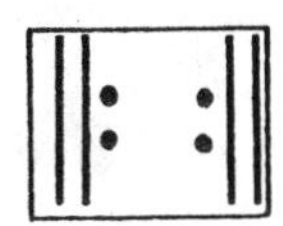

25. Oops card (same size and color as sign cards).

26. Whole-step cards (white, same size as alphabet cards) - Make five cards.

27. Half-step cards (red, same size as alphabet cards) - Make two cards.

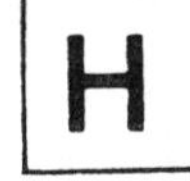

28. Key-signature cards -

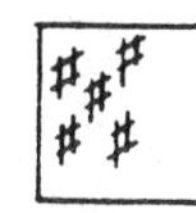

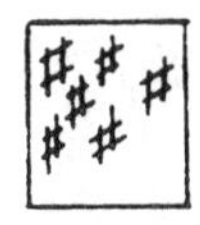

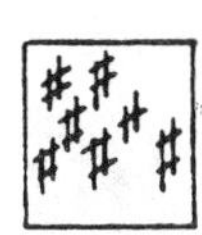

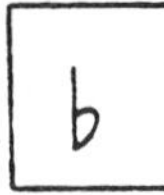

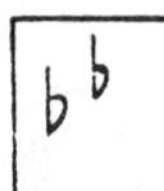

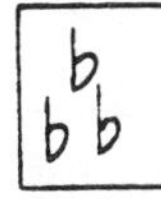

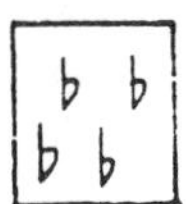

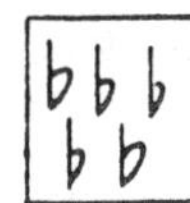

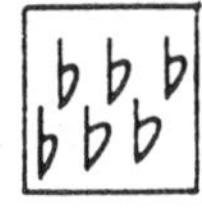

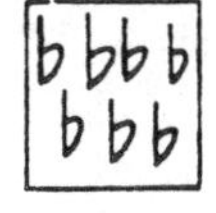

Music
Train

Music
Train

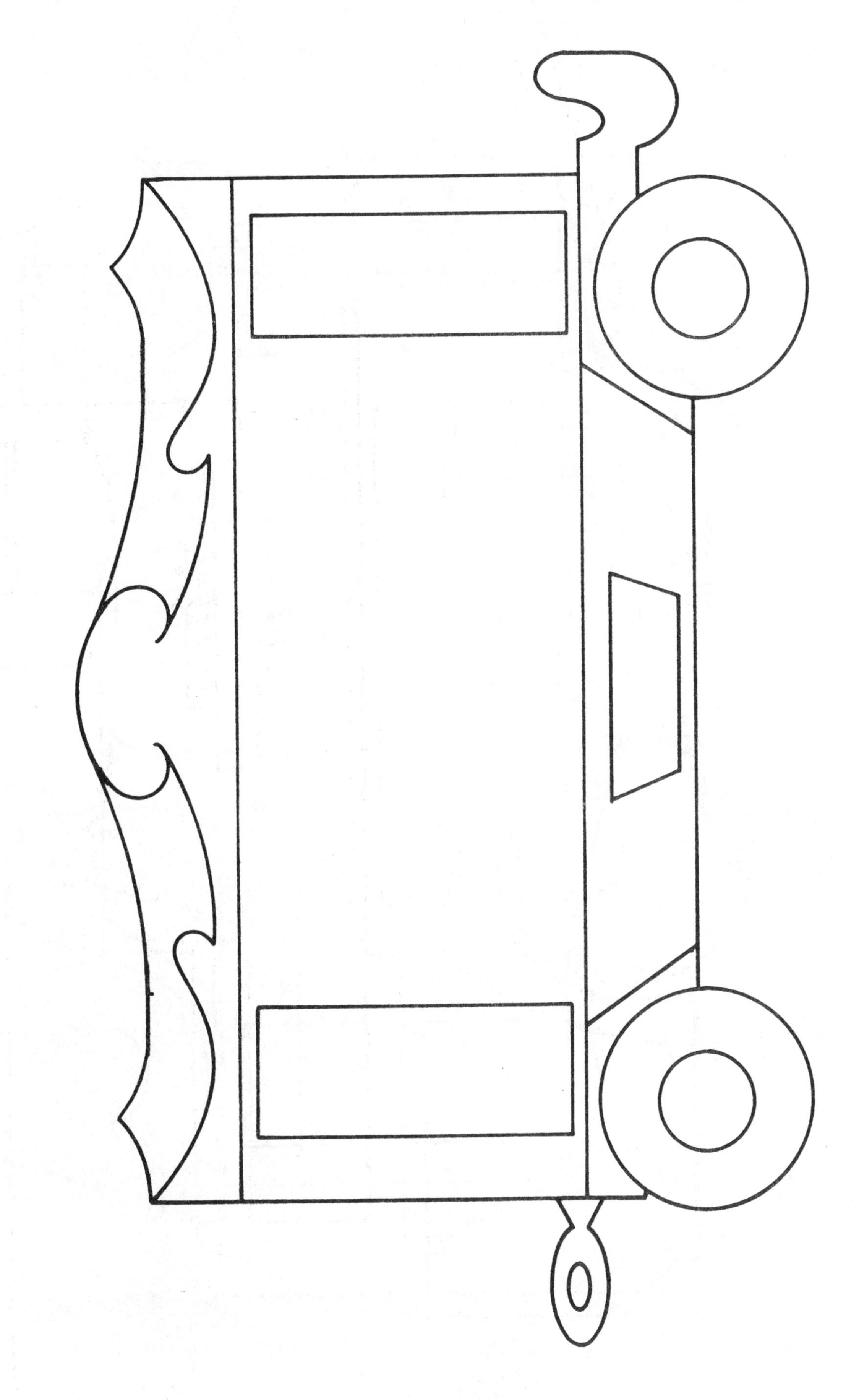

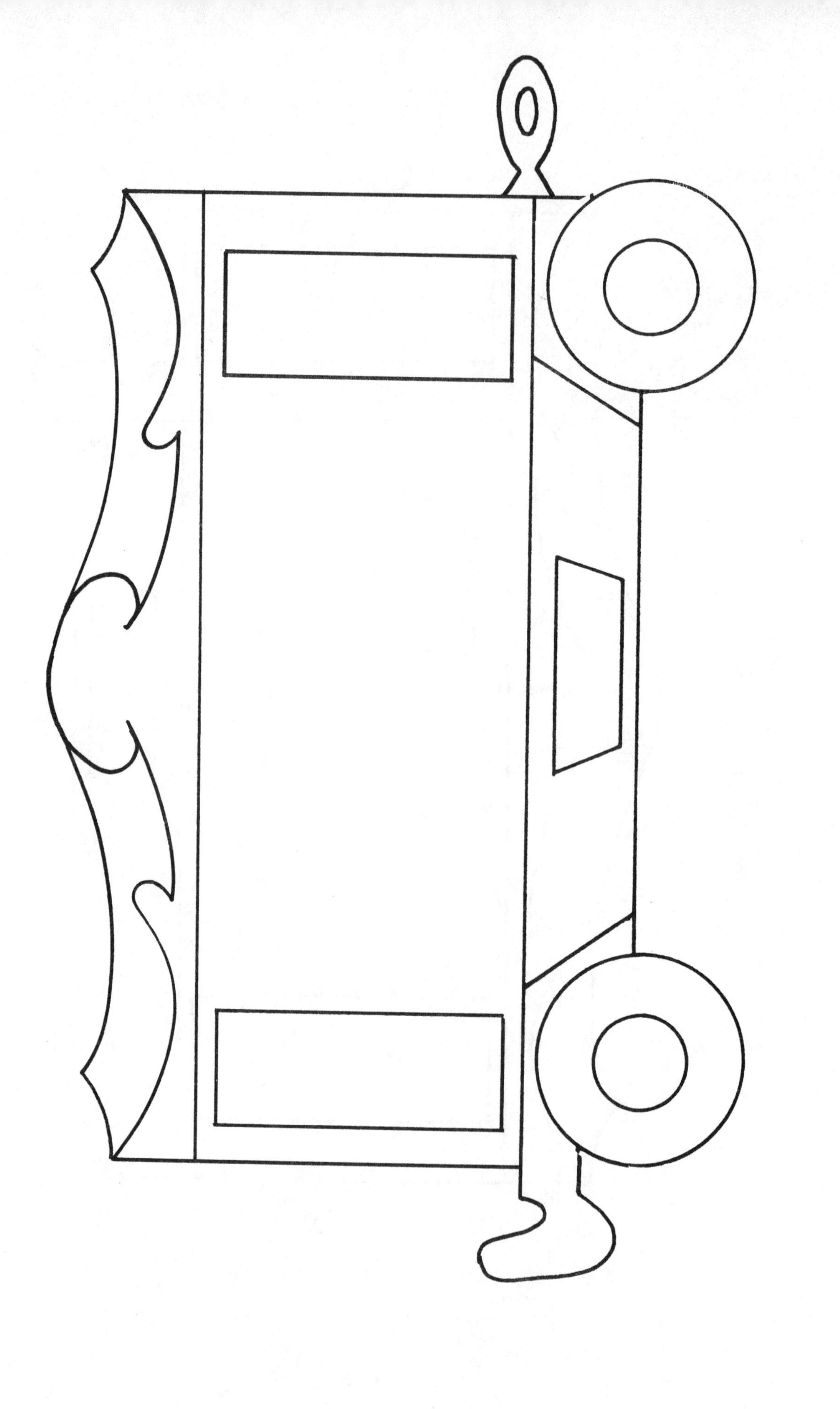

pp

p

mp

mf

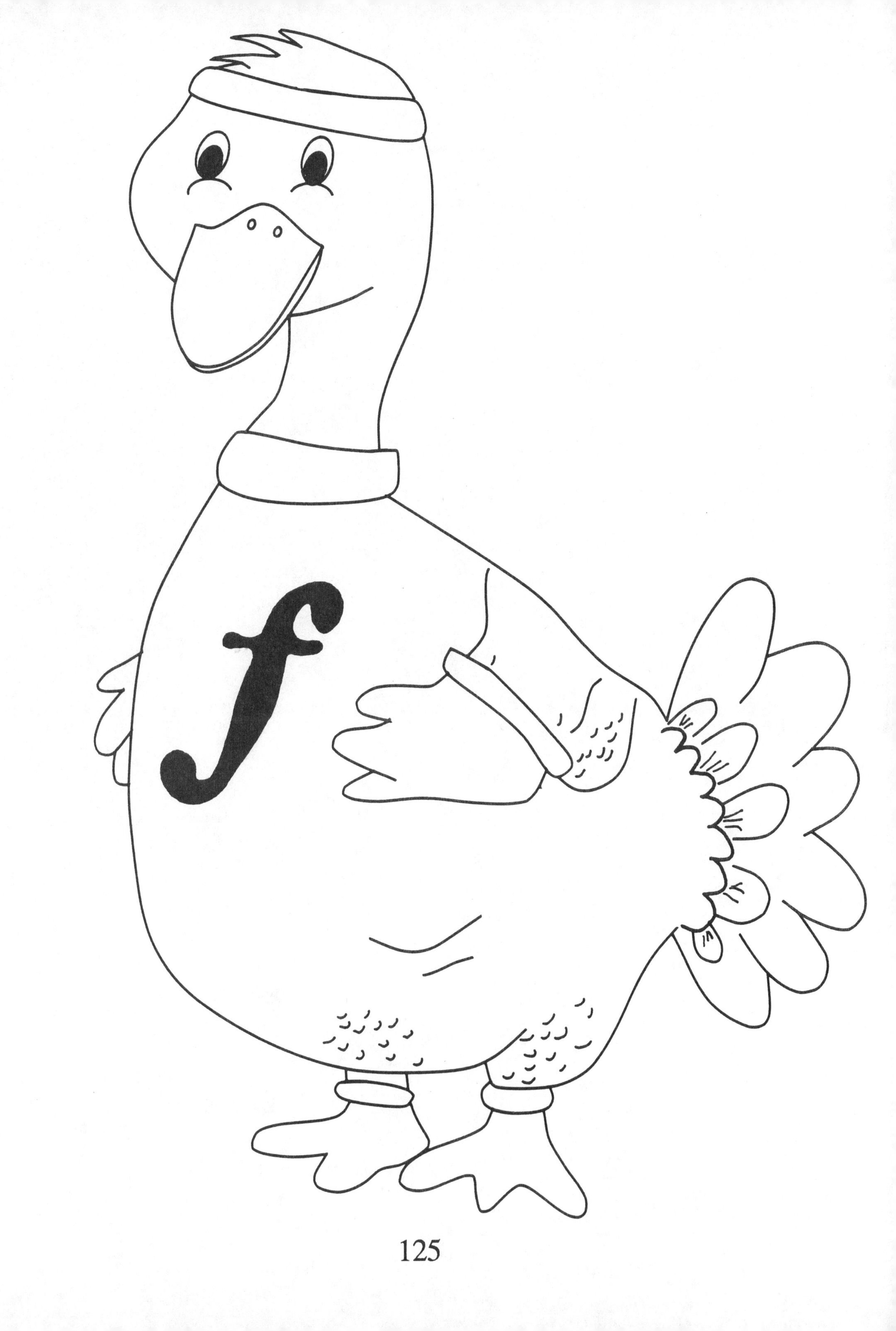
f

ff

Answer Key For Student Activities

Fun Page - Half Steps, page 38.

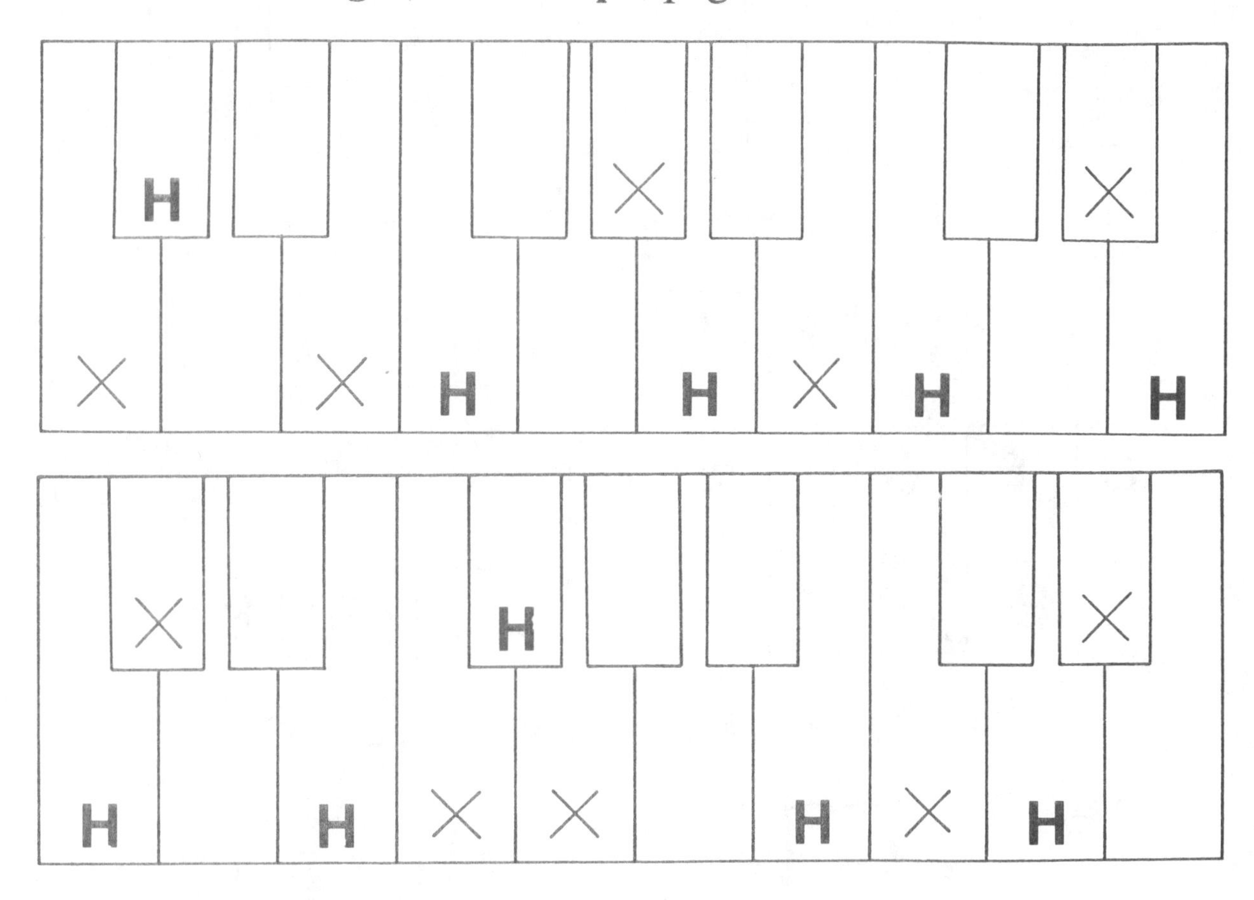

Fun Page - Whole Steps, page 40.

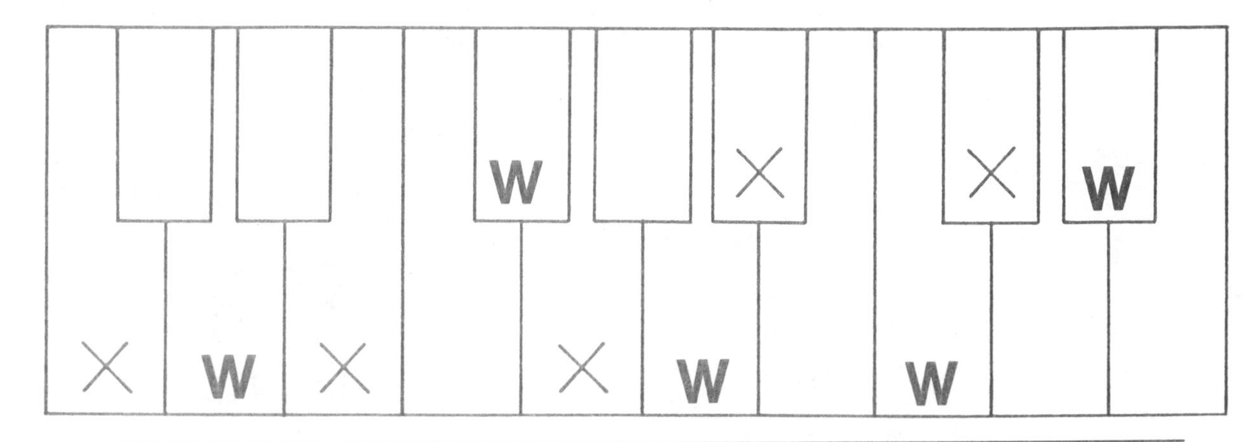

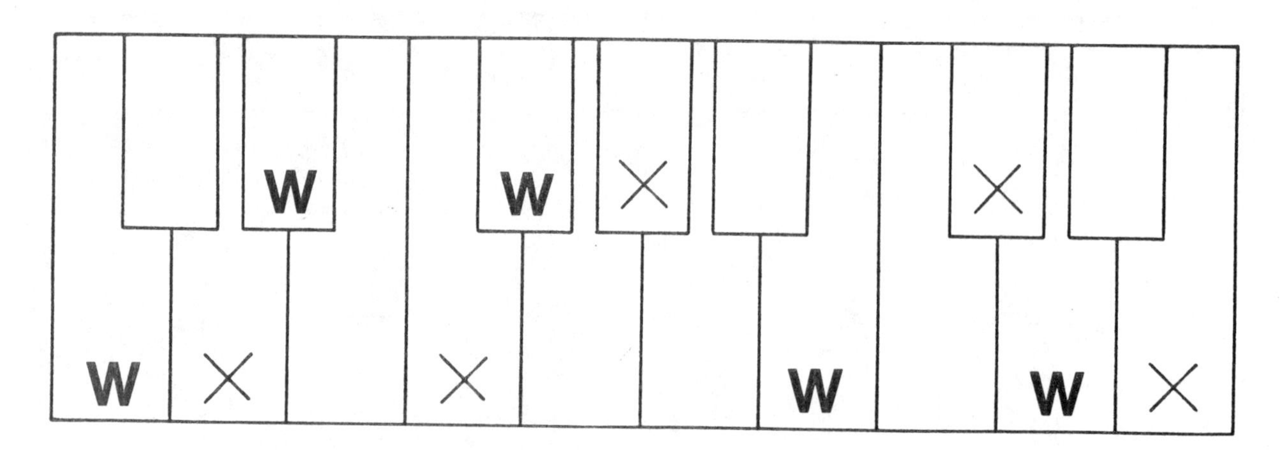

Spelling Triads, page 45.

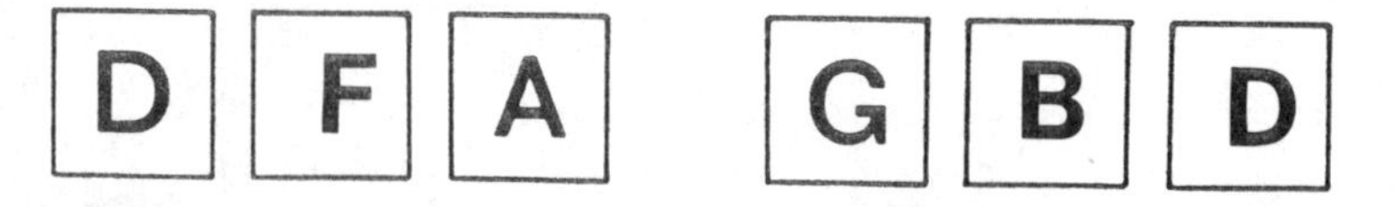

C E G A C E F A C

Fun Page - Triad Caterpillars, page 45.

A C E

C E G

D F A

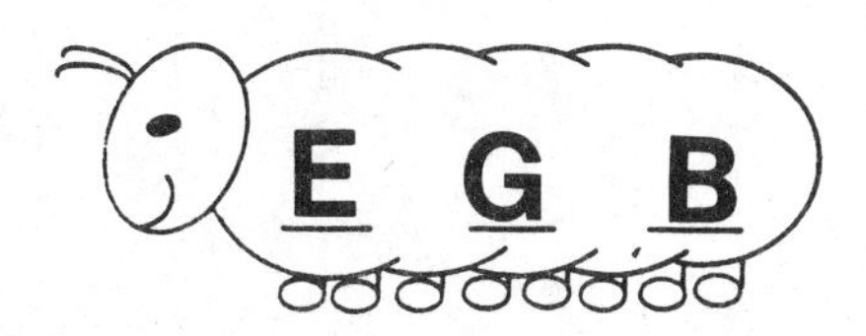
E G B

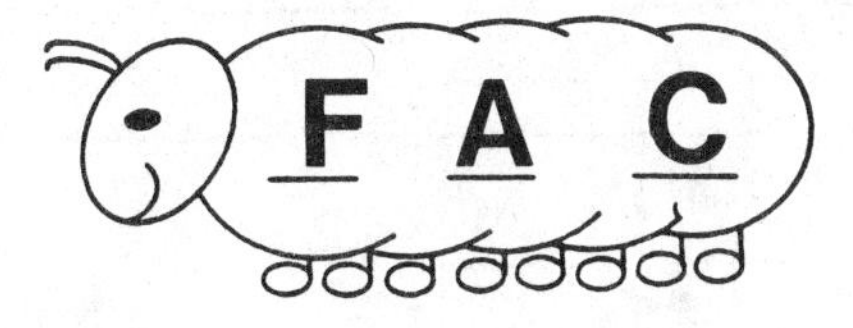
F A C

A C E

B D F

G B D

D F A

E G B

Fun Page - Note Identification, page 55.

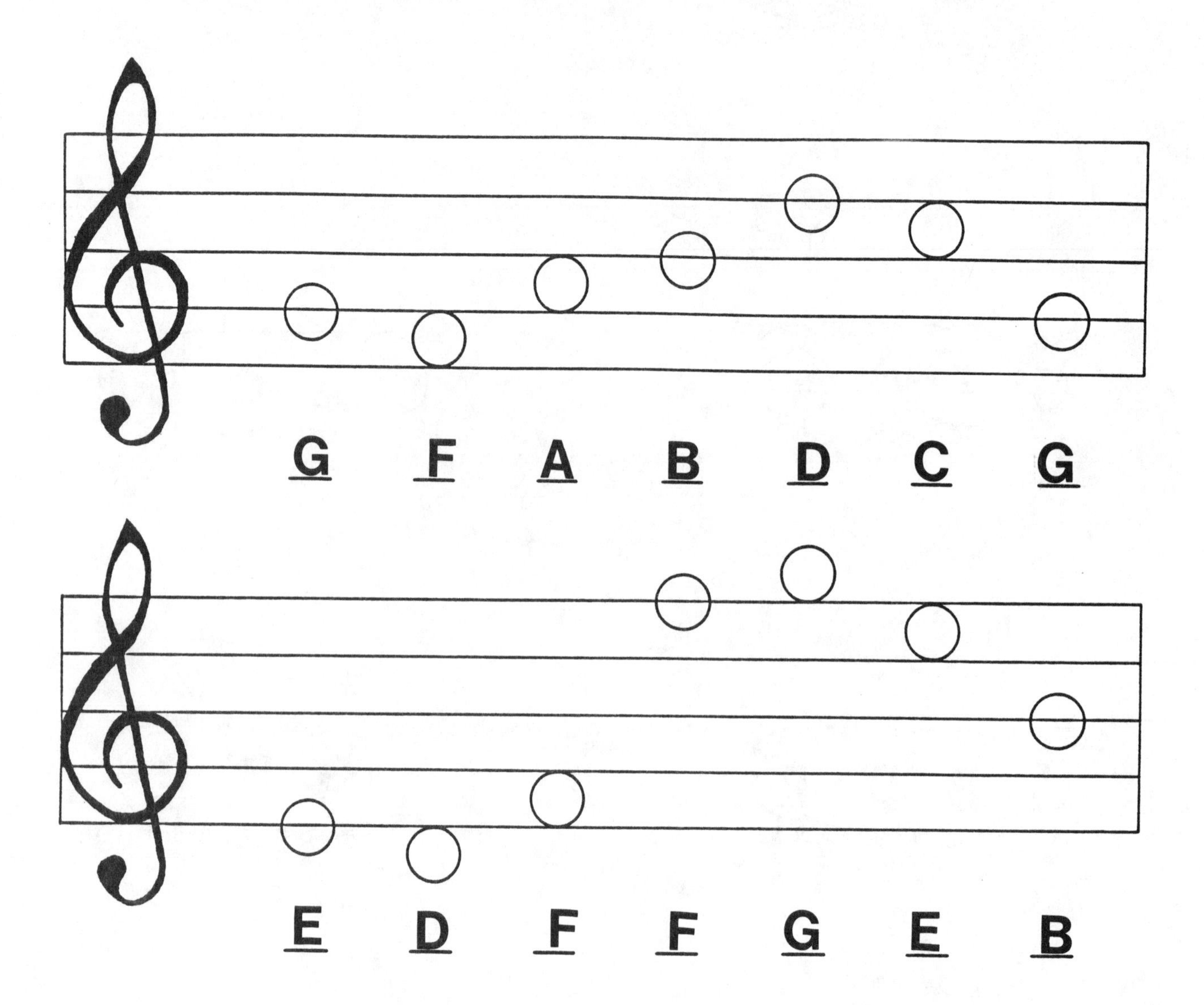

Fun Page - Treble Clef Notes, page 61.

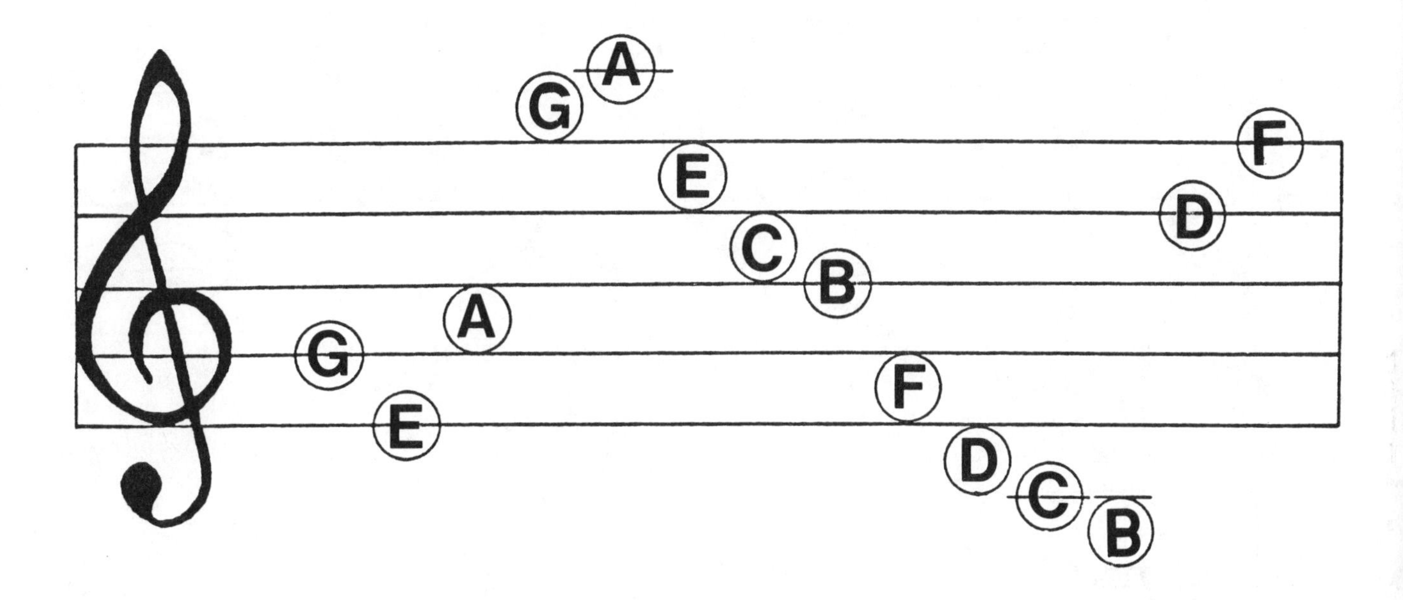

Fun Page - Bass Clef Trucks, page 62.

Fun Page - Bass Clef Notes, page 66.

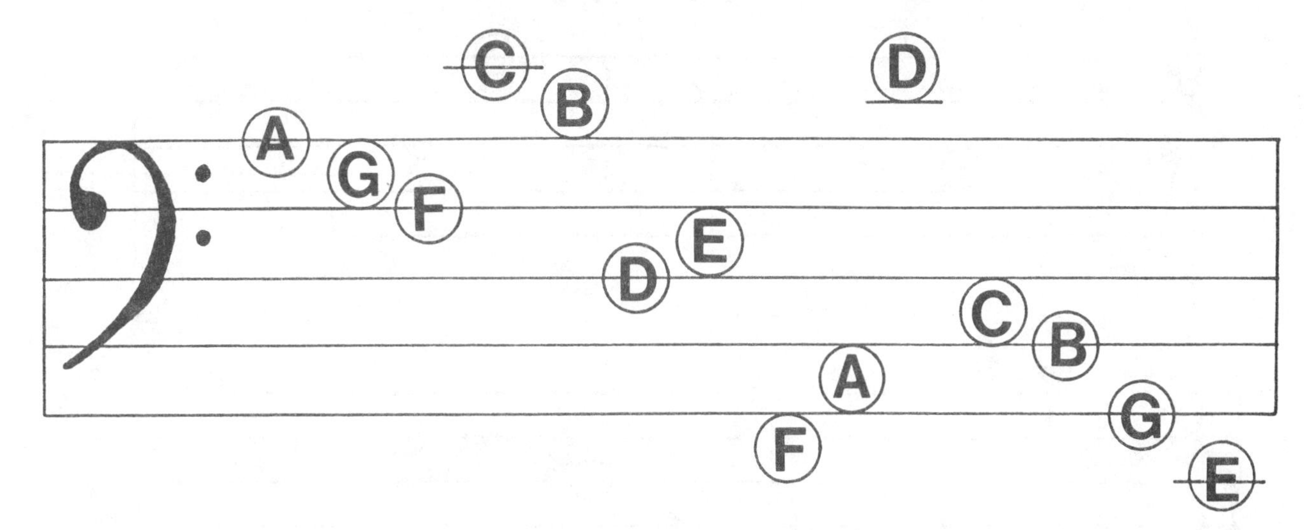

Focus on Key Signatures, page 95.

G	A	B	C	D	E	F#	G
D	E	F#	G	A	B	C#	D
A	B	C#	D	E	F#	G#	A
E	F#	G#	A	B	C#	D#	E
B	C#	D#	E	F#	G#	A#	B
F#	G#	A#	B	C#	D#	E#	F#
C#	D#	E#	F#	G#	A#	B#	C#

Fun Page - Major Scales I, page 98.

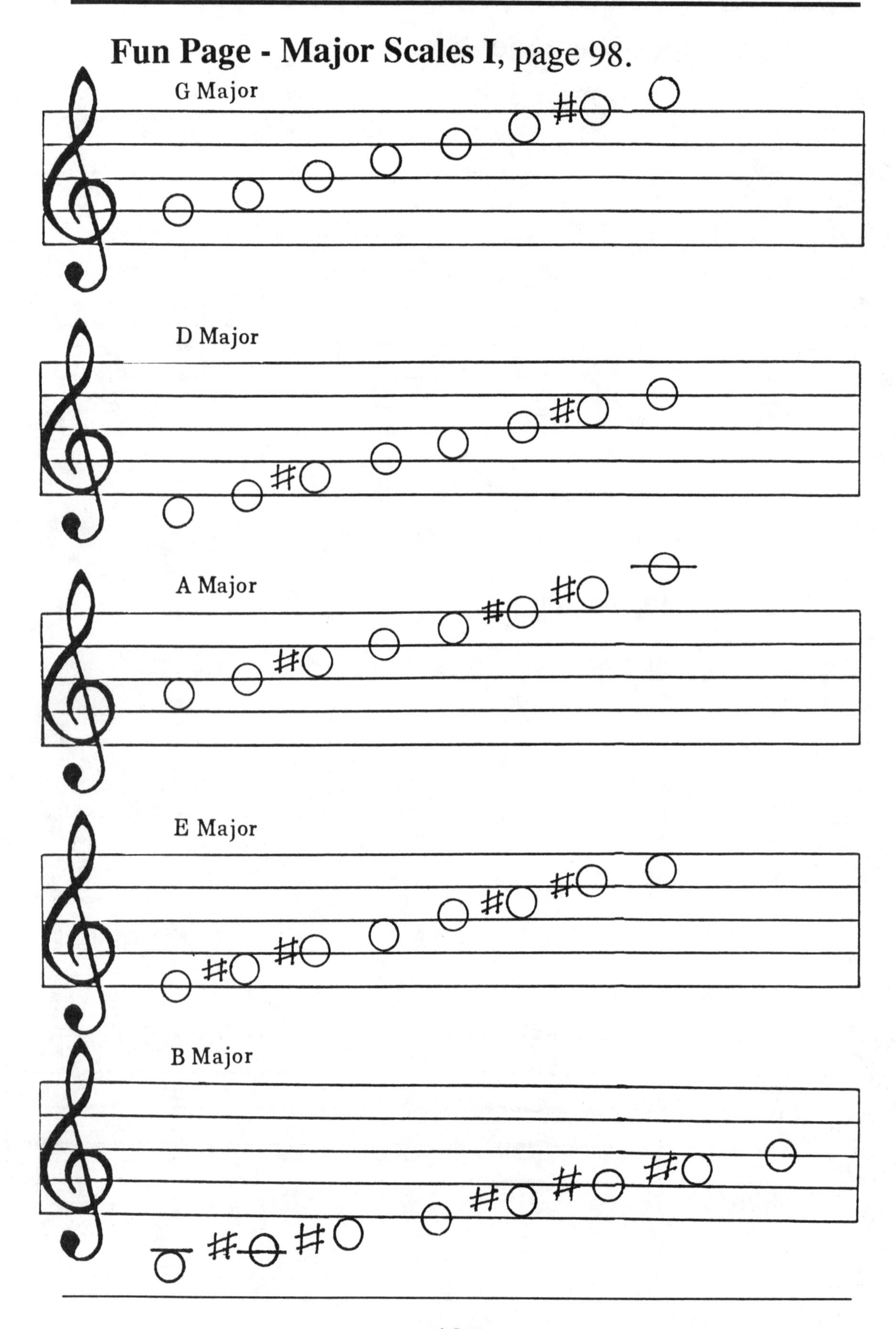

Fun Page - Key Signatures I, page 99.

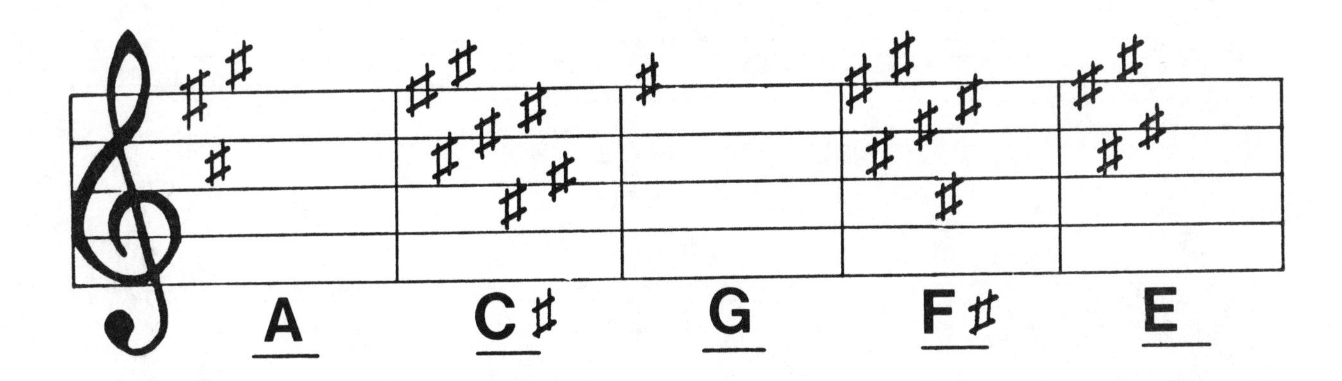

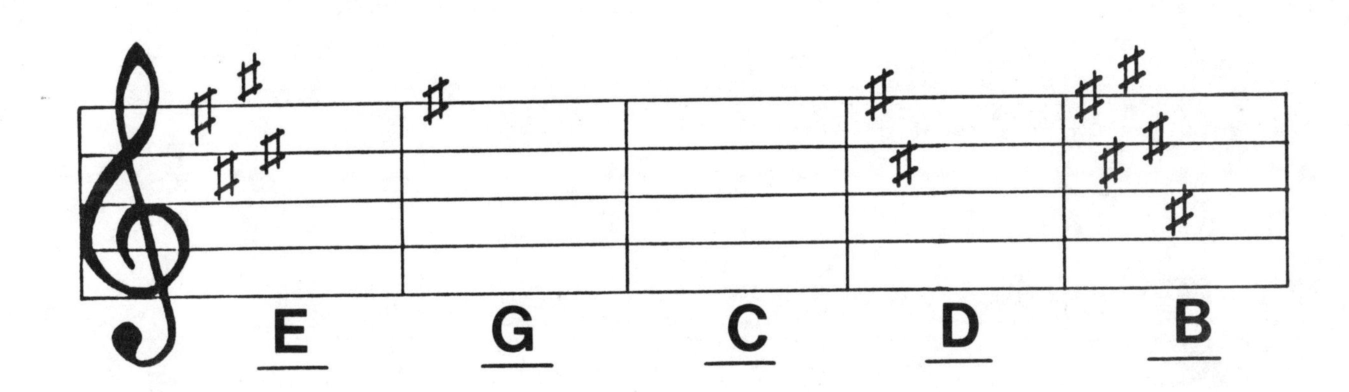

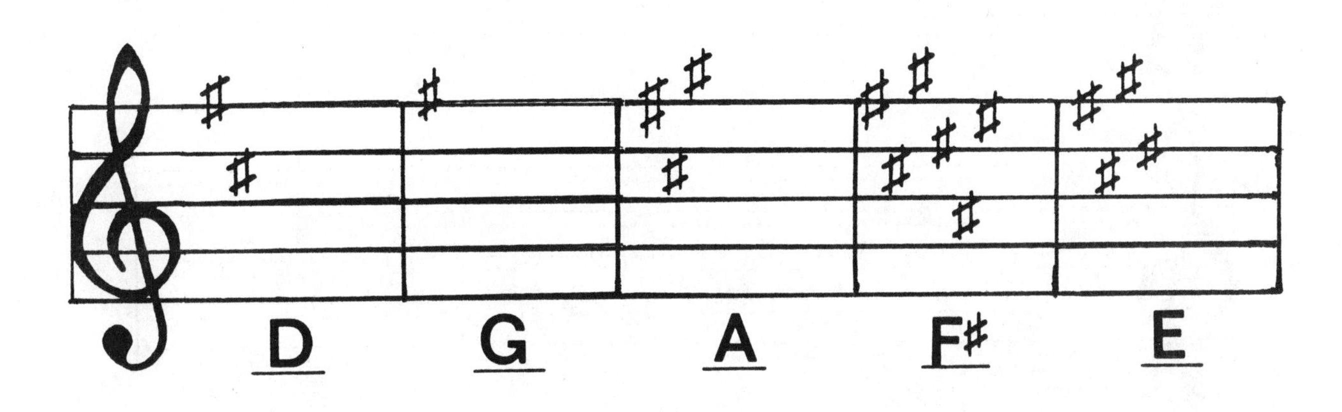

Fun Page - Major Scales II, page 102.

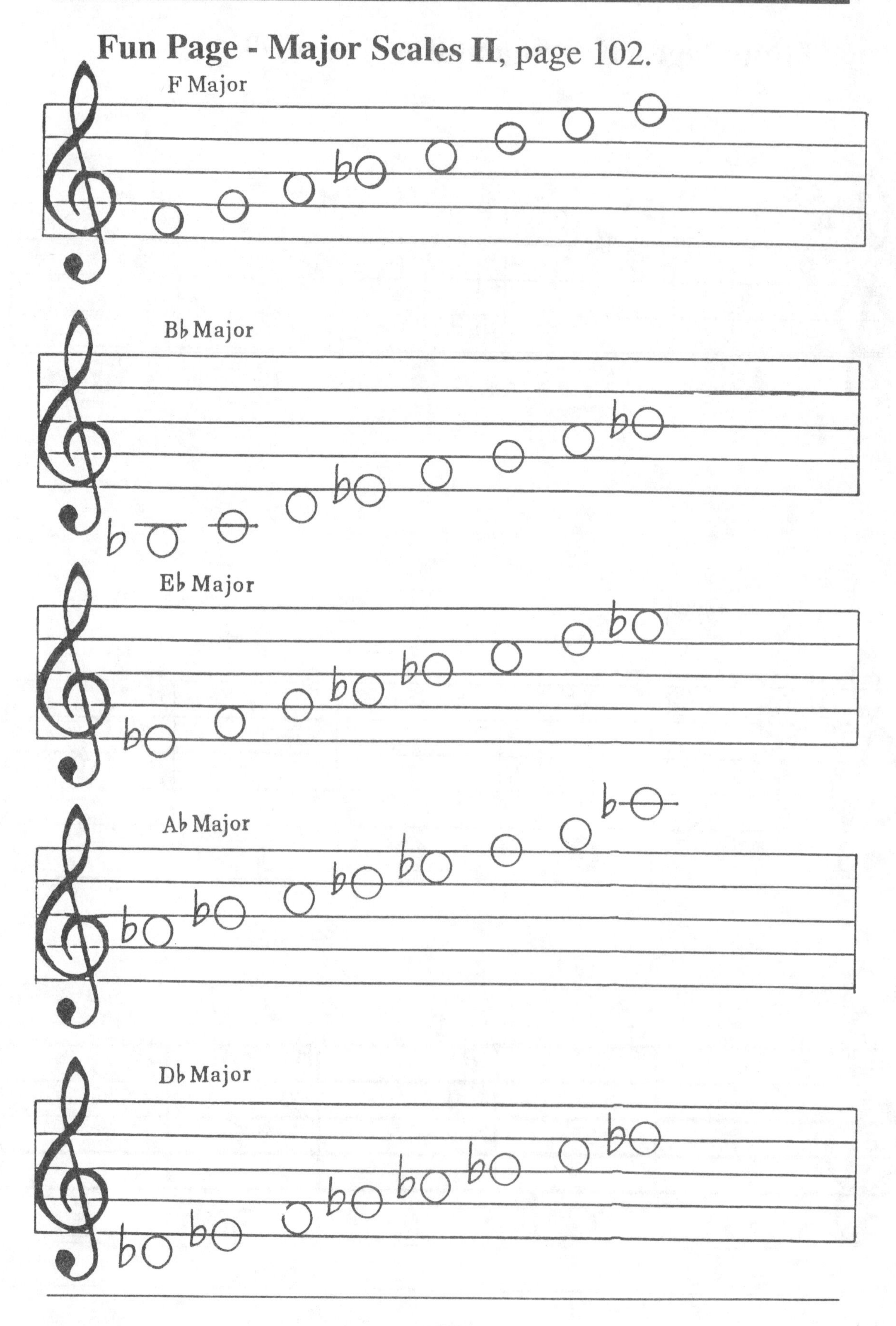

Fun Page - Key Signatures II, page 103.

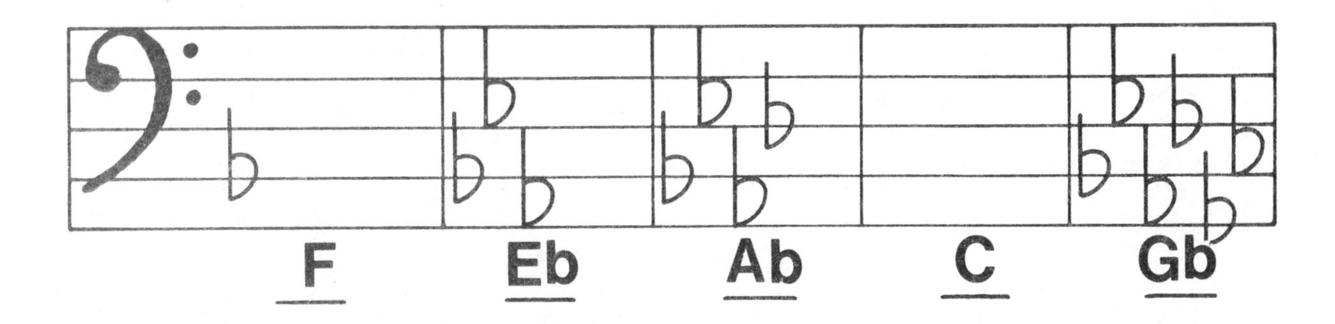

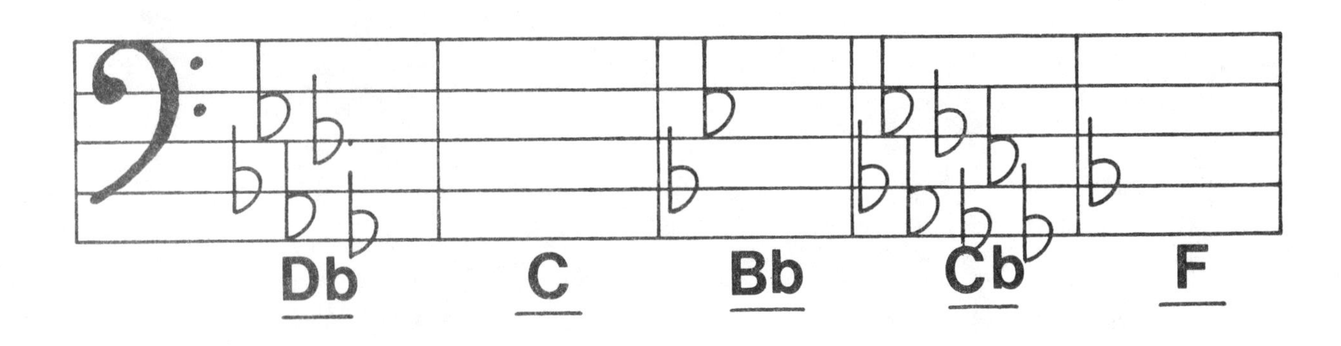

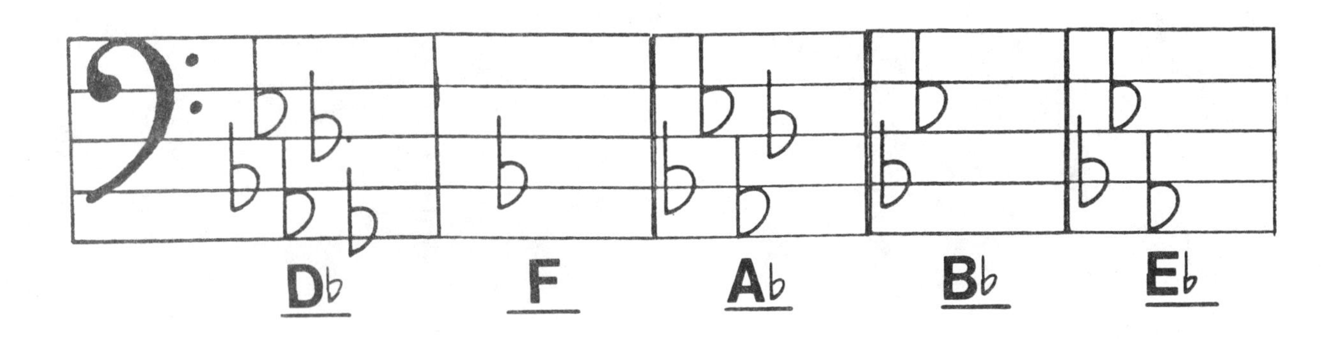

Now Available!

MANIPULATIVES KIT

FOR KEYBOARD CAPERS

Save preparation time with this fine quality manipulatives kit. This kit contains teaching aids for all of the games and activities found in Keyboard Capers. Each piece is professionally illustrated on heavy duty card stock and then laminated to withstand repeated use.

SEND ME:

☐ Manipulatives Kit...$39.95 + 3.50 shipping

☐ Unlaminated Manipulatives Kit.................................$20.00 + 2.50 shipping

(Tennessee residents add 8.25% sales tax.)

Please send me the books checked above:

Name: ______________________________

Street: ______________________________

City: ____________________ State ____________ Zip ________

ORDER NOW!

Checks may be made payable to:

Anne C. May

4435 Grindstone Ridge Rd.

Pigeon Forge, TN 37863

Allow 1 to 3 weeks for delivery.

Now Available!

MANIPULATIVES KIT

FOR KEYBOARD CAPERS

Save preparation time with this fine quality manipulatives kit. This kit contains teaching aids for all of the games and activities found in Keyboard Capers. Each piece is professionally illustrated on heavy duty card stock and then laminated to withstand repeated use.

SEND ME:

☐ Manipulatives Kit..........$39.95 + 3.50 shipping

☐ Unlaminated Manipulatives Kit..........$20.00 + 2.50 shipping

(Tennessee residents add 8.25% sales tax.)

Please send me the books checked above:

Name: ____________________

Street: ____________________

City: ____________ State ____________ Zip ____________

ORDER NOW!

Checks may be made payable to:

Anne C. May

4435 Grindstone Ridge Rd.

Pigeon Forge, TN 37863

Allow 1 to 3 weeks for delivery.

TO ORDER MORE COPIES OF KEYBOARD CAPERS:

Please send me _______copies of Keyboard Capers.
I am enclosing $18.95 per book, plus 10% (minimum of $2.50) for shipping & handling. Send payment to:

THE ELIJAH COMPANY
1053 ELDRIDGE LOOP
CROSSVILLE, TN 38555
1-888-235-4524

Name: ____

Address: ____

TO ORDER MORE COPIES OF KEYBOARD CAPERS:

Please send me _____copies of Keyboard Capers.
I am enclosing $18.95 per book, plus 10% (minimum of $2.50) for shipping & handling. Send payment to:

THE ELIJAH COMPANY
1053 ELDRIDGE LOOP
CROSSVILLE, TN 38555
1-888-235-4524

Name: ____

Address: ____

TO ORDER MORE COPIES OF KEYBOARD CAPERS:

Please send me ________copies of Keyboard Capers.
I am enclosing $18.95 per book, plus 10% (minimum of $2.50) for shipping & handling. Send payment to:

THE ELIJAH COMPANY
1053 ELDRIDGE LOOP
CROSSVILLE, TN 38555
1-888-235-4524

Name: ____

Address: ______________________________________

TO ORDER MORE COPIES OF KEYBOARD CAPERS:

Please send me ______copies of Keyboard Capers.
I am enclosing $18.95 per book, plus 10% (minimum of $2.50) for shipping & handling. Send payment to:

THE ELIJAH COMPANY
1053 ELDRIDGE LOOP
CROSSVILLE, TN 38555
1-888-235-4524

Name: ____

Address: ______________________________________